Girl on a Pony

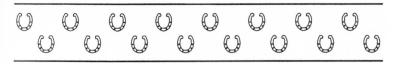

The Western Frontier Library

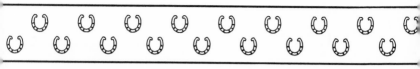

Girl on a

By LaVerne Hanners

University of Oklahoma Press
Norman and London

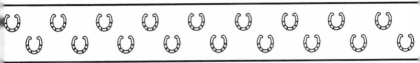

Pony

Frontispiece: LaVerne Hanners, age nineteen, up on Button. (Photo by Stella Goodson, Collection of LaVerne Hanners)

This book is published with the generous assistance of Edith Gaylord Harper.

Hanners, Laverne.
    Girl on a pony / by LaVerne Hanners. — 1st ed.
       p.   cm. — (The Western Frontier library ; v. 61)
    ISBN 0-8061-2624-8 (alk. paper)
          1. Hanners, Laverne — Homes and haunts — Oklahoma.
2. Women   poets,   American — 20th   century — Biography.
3. Hanners, Laverne — Childhood and youth.   4. Frontier and
pioneer life — Oklahoma.   5. Oklahoma — Social life and customs.   I. Title.   II. Series: Western frontier library ; 61.
PS3558.A4765Z466   1994
811'.54 — dc20
[B]   93-38833
                                                                 CIP

Girl on a Pony is Volume 61 in The Western Frontier Library.

The paper in this book meets the guidelines for permanence and durability of the Committee on Production Guidelines for Book Longevity of the Council on Library Resources, Inc. ∞

Text design by Cathy Imboden.

2   3   4   5   6   7   8   9   10

I dedicate *Girl on a Pony* to three stalwart western women:
    Stella Ellis Goodson, my mother
    Kathryn Belding Quimby, my teacher
    Marion Chadderdon Collins, my mother-in-law.

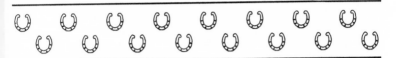

Contents

Contents

Illustrations

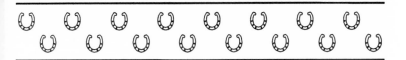

Maps

Acknowledgments

I would like to thank the Ball State University Forum for permission to publish the following material on which the Forum holds the copyright: three poems, "Can of Sad," "For Felix E. Goodson, Jr.," and "The Section Line," and parts of two prose articles, "The Horse in the Hotel" and "Cornmeal Living: the Women."

LaVerne Hanners holds the copyright on the following poems published in various magazines: "Mining Junk," "Foraging," and "DMZ" (retitled "Gardens") were published in the *Thornleigh Review*.

The poem, "A Lecture," was published in *Kites*. "The Shorthanded Branding," an article in a slightly longer version, was published in *The New Mexico Stockman*.

All of the above poems will soon be published in a book of poetry by LaVerne Hanners and Mary Patterson Thornburg. The book is named *Westering* and will be published by Lightning Tree Press in Boulder, Colorado, in 1993. Permission to publish the poems was granted earlier to Lightning Tree, which grants permission to reprint "A Lecture," "Gardens," and "Foraging."

I would also like to thank two incredible women who were able to type perfect copy from far less than perfect handwriting: Mary Patterson Thornburg and Jeanie Wyant. I am also extremely grateful to Dr. Thomas Oliver Mallory and Molly Mallory Johnson for proofreading the manuscript.

Girl on a Pony

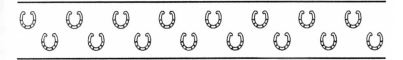

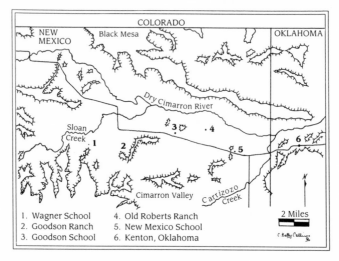

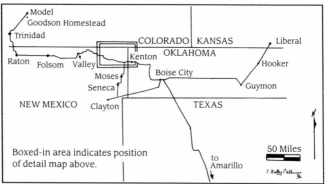

Map 1 (above), the Valley of the Dry Cimarron, natural habitat of the Goodson children and hunting ground of Jiggs Collins. Map 2 (below), shows the extreme isolation of the people of the Cimarron Valley, with shopping centers, doctors, and hospitals at punishing distances. The boxed-in area indicates the position of the detail map above. (Maps by C. Kelly Collins)

Chapter 1

The Country

I am a seeker of treasure. I look in thrift stores, junk sales, and auctions for the things that some dead mother's daughter threw away. I search for things my mother could have had and discarded. I look for my ancestral heritage in the Salvation Army. In Benton, Arkansas, at a booth in a flea market, I retrieved my youth.

I reached down between a pile of cooking utensils and a box of baby-food jars and brought out a stack of old photographs. I looked at the top picture on the stack and realized I was looking at a photograph of the Black Mesa—my childhood home. I bought all the pictures at once.

I have never stopped being homesick for that country—the Valley of the Dry Cimarron of New Mexico, and the flats beyond, the breaks that edge the Panhandle of Oklahoma on the west, the sky above the flats, the red dirt country, the meager river of the Cimarron, the little town of Kenton, Oklahoma—the country in the photographs. I even miss the storms, horrifying and deadly as they may sometimes be.

I make a journey every year. Each year I go back to that little town, and why I go I hardly know. I go over the Malpais Hill north and east of Clayton, New Mexico, and then head due north, driving too fast, but I am always in a hurry. When I finally see the thin, purple edge of the Black Mesa rising above the breaks, I slow my car. From these last high plains before the first foothills of the Rocky Mountains I can see the tip of Mount Capulin, sixty miles to the west, and Sierra Grande. I can see the top of the lone mesa behind our old home, perhaps twenty miles away. I drop down into the Cimarron Valley, turning east at the Y to cross the Carrizozo Creek into Oklahoma.

I make an abrupt right turn just before I drive into Kenton, and come to the gates of the cemetery on the west slope of the mesa above town. I drive into the cemetery along the west side and stop and get out. I always say that I need to come to check my father's grave, but that is only partly true. I come to this little cemetery each year to walk among the graves to count my friends and see which of those I knew in my childhood have been added to the roster.

My father's grave is in good order; the tombstone says only "Felix E. Goodson 1892–1936." The graves in this cemetery are always in good order. The trees are watered by the windmill in the northwest corner, and in the spring, when I come, the native grass is green.

In 1925 my family moved down from the claim in Colorado to a ranch in New Mexico. Kenton was a flourishing town just across the line in Oklahoma. It had two

Cora Wince and friend, with Black Mesa in the background. (Center for Southwest Research, General Library, University of New Mexico, 992–018)

banks, two garages, an ice-cream parlor, a hotel, a drugstore, and two grocery stores. Now, the town and the
country around it are almost deserted. Where once there
was a house on nearly every section, now there are only a
few ranch homes, or headquarters for large farms. There
are no schools left in the Valley. There is not a single
school from Boise City through Kenton and on up the
Valley past Folsom, a distance of more than one hundred
miles.

I drive back down the short side road and into Kenton. Sometimes I stop in the one business establishment
left, the old general store built by D. K. and Ed Lord and
known then as Lord's Store. It seems much smaller now,
and I can't imagine where they kept all the merchandise I
remember seeing there long ago.

The bridles hung back in the southeast corner. Mother
let me keep the egg money one month so I could buy a
bridle. I wanted that bridle more than anything. My two
brothers, John and Felix, had bridles, and John even had a
small saddle, but I had to ride with a rope hackamore. I
hunted eggs and gathered eggs and begrudged every one
my mother cooked, but I finally had the five dollars I
needed. I was rarely proud of that bridle. One of the
cowboys made fun of it, saying, "This leather is like
paper. You could have bought five dollars worth of leather, and I could have made you a good bridle."

I didn't say anything. How could I? I was eight years
old and he was a cowboy. I didn't realize how much I
resented his criticism of my bridle until fifty years later. I
had bought a new truck, red and powerful. I loved that
truck. Some man asked me what I had paid for it, and like
a fool I told him. He said, "My God, I've got a cousin who

Lord's Store, side and front views, 1989. (Photos by LaVerne Hanners, Collection of LaVerne Hanners)

has a dealership. He could have got that truck two thousand dollars cheaper.''

I was so angry that I saw a red haze before my eyes, and in that haze I saw a bridle. I screamed at him. ''Well, where was your goddamn cousin when I really needed him? I can't stand some smartass man who tells me how much better and cheaper he could have done something, especially," I added cruelly, "when that man is hitching a ride to work every morning." I went on from that, getting louder and louder, until my granddaughter got her hand over my mouth. Every man should take notice that he should never, never tell a woman, especially a western woman, how much cheaper and easier he could have done something. Somewhere in her past that woman may have a bridle for which she scrimped and saved.

I always drive a circle around the streets of Kenton. I notice the houses that have been torn down, and am again surprised to see that the flags still grow where I planted them fifty years ago when I first lived in Kenton and was married to Jiggs Collins. The house is gone, of course. It was nearly gone when we lived in it. It was just a shack, really, but it was the first home I had that was my own, and the house we brought Sandy back to when she was born.

When Sandy was three years old Jiggs and I moved over the state line to New Mexico, where we became pig farmers. We were sharecropping the pigs. Jiggs and his younger brother David had entered into an agreement with Meredith Hughes to become with him the Pig Barons of the Cimarron. Meredith was putting up the money, and the boys were doing all the labor.

Jiggs and I, and David and Winifred, moved onto the Hughes place, and we all started raising hogs. The boys circled the countryside buying weanlings, shoats, gilts, and pregnant sows. They went up into Colorado and Kansas, and out into the Oklahoma and Texas panhandles. They bought every hog that walked and brought all

Bank building, Kenton, Oklahoma, 1923 (Center for Southwest Research, General Library, University of New Mexico, 992–018)

those hogs back to Meredith's ranch and put them out into the alfalfa fields.

The pregnant sows, fourteen enormous Berkshires, went into the adobe hog barn. They farrowed almost simultaneously, having from ten to fourteen pigs apiece. Then the rains came.

During one of those unusual years when it really rained in New Mexico, it rained and rained and rained in Union County. I believe that the official measurement was about three times the average. New Mexico just wasn't built to take that kind of moisture. Great cracks opened in the mesas, whole hillsides suddenly slipped, the Dry Cimarron River widened its banks in some places by a hundred feet, and our adobe hog barn dissolved.

The men rushed out to the barn, snatched little pigs out of the mud, and made a running trip by the horse tank, where they sloshed the pigs around a bit in the water to get most of the mud off them. Then they handed the pigs to Winifred and me and rushed off for more.

Winnie and I scrubbed and rubbed the pigs with towels, old sheets, and the tablecloth and laid them in the oven like cordwood. The poor little porkers were absolutely limp when they were brought in, but they didn't stay that way. As soon as the warmth from the oven began to percolate through their little insides, they came alive. When one started reviving we snatched him out of the oven, set him on the floor, and replaced him with a newly rescued one. The kitchen was soon alive with pigs in various stages of activity. The floor was inches deep in mud. The pigs were running in and out among the chairs, squealing like bagpipes, and Winnie and I were nearing nervous breakdown.

Finally the men came in. "Well, I guess that's all," one of them said.

"Oh, fine," I said. "Now let's get these pigs out of here so we can clean the kitchen."

The men looked astonished. Jiggs said, "Now, La-Verne, we can't do that. We don't have any place to put them. We'll have to leave them in here tonight and try to fix a place for them up on the hill tomorrow."

We saved all those baby pigs and got them back to their mothers, who had been put in hastily constructed wire pens. The rains finally stopped, the hogs were flourishing, and for a good few weeks it seemed that we were on our way to a meager prosperity.

Jiggs and David had put forty shoats in the fattening pen and stuffed them with all the food they could eat. The pigs were gobby fat, as was the custom in those days of unknown cholesterol counts. Besides, this was during the war, when every drop of oil of any kind was precious. The men were leaning on the fence looking at the pigs when Jiggs said, "Look there, David. See that Poland China over in the corner? Does he look okay to you?"

"I think he's just asleep." David tossed a clod of dirt that smacked the pig in the face. The pig twitched his front legs.

Jiggs climbed over the fence and delivered a hearty kick to the pig's rump. The Poland China wearily struggled to a sitting position and propped himself on his front legs. He sat there swaying back and forth.

"That pig's sick," David said.

"Cholera," Jiggs groaned. "I told Meredith we had to vaccinate these pigs." Indeed, there had been quite an argument about it, but Meredith was old-fashioned. He had raised pigs all his life, and his daddy before him, and had never had any trouble. And Meredith had the money. We didn't have a penny.

To do Meredith justice, cholera had never been a problem in the area, and no one ever vaccinated pigs. The pigs on most ranches were grown for meat and lard for the family. The brood sows were kept back from litters, and the only time a strange hog would have been around was when a boar was brought over for breeding.

The Poland China died that night, and by morning seven more were sick. Then the nightmare began in earnest.

Meredith took one look at the pigs and promptly got drunk. He did furnish the money to send to Springfield for a veterinarian and vaccine. The vet came, and Meredith with his somewhat impaired judgment insisted he vaccinate the sick pigs first. Jiggs drove to Amarillo and bought all the vaccine there, and as he came back he stopped at all the towns on the way and bought their vaccine.

Then the sick pigs died, taking with them the only vaccine within a radius of three hundred miles.

Jiggs, David, and Meredith drove to Denver, stopping at every town in between. They weren't able to get much, and that stands to reason. If a distraught-looking man came pelting in demanding all of the hog cholera vaccine in the drugstore, the druggist would surely hold some back for regular customers, just in case there was a widespread epidemic. Whatever the reason, the men exhausted the supply of available vaccine, and still pigs continued to die. As they died, Jiggs or David hooked them to the tractor and dragged them up to the foot of the Black Mesa and shoved them in a small arroyo. In the hot

sun of summer, liquid lard ran down that arroyo in rivu-
lets. A sickening stench filled the air, and buzzards circled above the ranch for weeks.

A man who had immigrated from some mid-European
country many years before told Jiggs of a remedy they
used back in the old country. They must, he said, roast the
dead hogs and feed the carcasses to the living. There
were about a hundred pigs left by then. Jiggs and David
were so desperate they tried it. They built a huge bonfire
and threw the dead pigs on it. Then they chopped up the
bodies with axes and fed them to the pigs that were left.

It didn't work, of course, and the men went through
that medieval ordeal for nothing. I have been informed
that the reasoning behind that nightmarish activity was
basically sound. The bonfires would have killed the cholera bacteria, and the killed bacteria should have acted as
an immunization agent. Our pigs were probably already
infected when subjected to that bizarre remedy, but the
idea wasn't absolutely insane. As I write I realize that
there is much I do not know about hog cholera or health
laws then or now. We must surely have been in violation
of many laws from many states, but we didn't know it
then, and I don't want to know it now.

The last of the pigs but one died, and the afternoon
that Jiggs dragged that pig up to the Mesa, Meredith asked
David and him down to the ranch house for a drink.
Meredith broke out a new bottle of Black and White
scotch and the three men sat on the porch solemnly
passing the bottle back and forth among them.

Meredith laid his head back and dozed off while Jiggs
and David continued to punish the scotch. Suddenly Meredith's eyes snapped open. An old sow, the sole survivor

of the cholera, came wobbling out of the barn. Meredith went into his house and came out with his rifle. He took careful aim and shot the sow between the eyes. "Well," Meredith said, "That's one son of a bitch the cholera won't get."

Jiggs fired up the tractor again to drag the old sow off, and we went out of the hog business.

Sometimes a panic hits me when I drive around Kenton. If there are too many new names on the slope, and if there are too many ghosts lingering around the sad little town, then I drive, again too fast, back across the state line into New Mexico on the dirt road up the Cimarron Valley. I drive past our old ranch on the left against the south mesas, but I do not look in that direction. I drive a hundred miles to Raton, then to Santa Fe.

There came a summer when I drove back to Kenton, and that time I stayed a while. I had found the photographs by then and knew that I wanted to write about them and the people in them and about my family and all the other families who had lived in the tar-paper shacks and half-dugouts on the homesteads.

The map of the Panhandle of Oklahoma looks very neat and tidy. There are the straight lines where it is joined to New Mexico on the west, to Texas on the south, and to Colorado and Kansas on the north. In actual fact, the country is not that simple. The Black Mesa winds from west to east, down from the rugged volcano country of Folsom and Capulin in New Mexico, and ends just a few miles inside of Oklahoma. The Mesa ends abruptly, like a stalled locomotive, towering hundreds of feet up from the valley floor. The summit there at the end is the highest point in Oklahoma.

New Mexico has two Cimarron rivers. One flows down the Cimarron Valley at the north edge of New Mexico. It heads above Folsom and joins the Arkansas River at Tulsa. The other Cimarron heads at Eagle Nest Lake, flows down the Cimarron Canyon and through the town of Cimarron, and joins the Canadian River at Taylor Springs.

I am sure the first explorers thought they were the same, the two rivers that they named Cimarron, to the confusion of everyone thereafter. The people of the Valley where I lived began calling our river the Dry Cimarron to differentiate between the two. I cannot find that designation on any map, so I imagine New Mexico may be the only state with two separate rivers with the same name. The Dry Cimarron River parallels the Black Mesa in New Mexico and in Oklahoma, flowing on past Kenton into the last few breaks before it heads on down the Panhandle. The breaks end at the 101 Hill. One tops out there, and from there on to the end of the Panhandle, and beyond, lie the high plains of Oklahoma. The residents of the plains are fascinated with the western end of the Panhandle. The upthrust of the Black Mesa, the canyons, and the strange rock formations are a change to those used to rolling plains and vast horizons. They come to these breaks for vacations, to camp and to climb. In 1922 a woman named Cora Wince came to Kenton with her family and friends. They took photographs and climbed and posed on the rocks. Those photographs of the Black Mesa and the surrounding country were the ones I picked up in the flea market.

The Black Mesa is capped by the malpais rock formed by the cooling lava that flowed down the Cimarron mil-

Bess Fox and Lewis Barton on Black Mesa with a live rattler, June 11, 1922. (Center for Southwest Research, General Library, University of New Mexico, 992–018)

lennia ago. Under the malpais cliff is another cliff of sandstone. One can look across the Valley and see the same sandstone capping the mesas of the south. The south side of the Valley is rougher than the north side and more broken, with lone mesas carved out by the weather and with deeper canyons. The malpais cap has protected the Black Mesa from the weathering, and it rises mono-lithic and somber from the Valley floor without a break or natural pass for sixty miles or more.

Except for the cottonwoods along the banks of the Cimarron the only trees in the Valley are a few orchards and elms around the homes, and of course the evergreen, ever-present scrub cedar and piñon, and the scrub oak on the slopes. The Valley's floor is covered with cane cactus, prickly pear, and soapweed. I suppose it looks desolate to outsiders, but the natives of the Valley and the plains to the east are always shocked to hear them say so. I took a young girl with me once when I went back home to the Valley. Francine didn't say much, but when we got back to Arkansas she jumped out of the pickup and ran into her house to say to her mother, "Mama, there weren't but two trees in that whole country, and they were both leaning sideways."

I can imagine how the Valley and the wide plains must appear to someone used to the subtropics of Arkan-sas. The prevailing winds on the plains are from the southwest, and the trees do, indeed, lean sideways. Ar-kansas, to the native of the plains and mesas, seems overgrown. I feel like my eyes are trapped and like every-where I look I am looking directly into the trunk of a tree. It is such a relief to see the plains. As soon as I leave the Ozarks and hit the rolling hills of central Oklahoma, I set my eyes free and look into distance. I can see a thunder-head pouring rain twenty miles away and can judge accurately if it will come toward me. In Arkansas, storms hide behind trees and pop out without any warning. But in New Mexico—even in the Valley, where the view is limited—one can look up the Cimarron and see the clouds building, or look to the north and see distant rain on the slopes of the Black Mesa.

The Valley, although cut by the state line, is one community. From the Cross L ranch out of Folsom and on down the river past Kenton, this community is bound together by the terrain. The Valley begins above Folsom, with the headwaters of the Cimarron, and goes east, becoming wider in places and almost closed in others.

The people of the community are joined together by the churches at Kenton and, perhaps more than any other thing, the cemetery above Kenton. There the Likes are buried, and Felix Goodson. The Giles and Wiggins and Quimby families are there from the New Mexico ranches west of the line, along with the Collinses, Labriers, and Brookharts from Oklahoma. There are graves of persons from up on the Colorado flats. Funeral corteges wind down the Valley: they come from Clayton, from Boise City, and from Springfield, Colorado, to bring the dead back to Kenton as their natural resting place. They do not sell the plots at Kenton cemetery. Burial is free, and until recently the graves were dug by neighbors.

There were other bonds between the states. The young men from the towns of Kenton and Boise City went up the Valley as cowboys on the ranches, and the ranchers' sons went out on the plains to help the farmers with harvest. There were romances and marriages across the line, and always there was the shopping, the going into Kenton to get mail or send a package and to buy food and chicken feed at Lord's Store. We shipped eggs and cream from Kenton and shopped among the bolts of dress material. I think sometimes we just went to visit, to exchange conversation with the others who had crowded into the little post office to wait for the mail to be put up.

The man who carried the mail from Clayton was a vital link to the world of hardware and dry-goods stores, to any store that sold merchandise not carried in Kenton. The mail carrier shopped for us all and brought us medicines, clothing, and all manner of things available in Clayton. Once when the Easleys owned the store and ran the post office, Estelle Easley sent to Herztein's in Clayton for a new corset. Ralph Bullard was carrying the mail then. He came in the door of the store waving the pink garment by the laces. He yelled to the back of the store, where Estelle was working on the books, "Hey, Estelle, I got your corset. I know it's going to fit. I tried it on a sack of potatoes just before I left town."

The carriers also hauled passengers. This was an essential service, especially during the war, when gasoline was severely rationed. We went on the mail truck to see doctors and to shop, going in in the afternoon and coming back the next morning.

The state line did occasion some division. There were separate schools, and there were different politics. The Union County seat is at Clayton, and Boise City is the county seat of Cimarron County. In the areas of schools and government the states were distinct and apart. It did not seem to make much difference. If Kenton put on a box supper to raise money for the school, everyone came, and if there was a social event of any kind across the New Mexico line, the people came from Kenton.

The community was also united by the weather. The floods that roar out of the canyons of the upper valley go racing on past Kenton, taking the bridges with them. In Arkansas sometimes I would see a flash flood warning on television, and I wanted to yell, "Man, you don't know a thing about flash floods!" The water rises in Arkansas; in the Cimarron Valley it comes down like a moving wall. If there is a heavy rain back up the canyons, small dry creeks and arroyos become torrents of water, all converging on the one outlet, the Cimarron. The waters, meeting there, uproot cottonwood trees and bring them tumbling and boiling, along with the piles and timbers from the Layton bridge. This roaring mass hits the pilings of the Wiggins bridge, adds them to the debris, goes on down the river for a few miles, and takes out the Tucker bridge.

Perhaps the bridges are better built now. Maybe the men do not now have to go out to the river where they know of a rock bottom and scrape a road up through the new cut banks to make a ford. Maybe. But I know the Cimarron. Men perhaps can build a better bridge, but if the Cimarron really floods it can take out any of them.

Probably meteorologists know why the storms in the area around the northeastern corner of New Mexico are so malevolent. It must have to do with prevailing winds, high altitude, longitude, and bad luck. To the residents of the area the weather seems like a personal enemy. Freakish storms wait in ambush. Cloudbursts lurk in the beautiful, fluffy cumulus clouds. Blizzards drop over the Black Mesa, and hailstorms attack from every direction.

One flood was so devastating that it was given its own name, the Great Folsom Flood. Its history has been recorded in a little booklet about Folsom, New Mexico. On August 27, 1908, there was a cloudburst above Folsom. A rancher upriver watched in horror as a wall of water took his barn and corrals. The rancher ran to his telephone and called the switchboard operator in Folsom. The operator's name was Sarah Rooke. She began calling ranchers downriver, warning the people to get out and up the hill. She saved many lives but was not able to save her own. She still had her headphone on when the water struck the telephone office and swept it and her away. Her body was not found for nearly a year. Two cowboys, sawing up a pile of driftwood for kindling, mistook her mummified body for driftwood and were about to saw it up when they realized they were handling a human body.

At my house in Arkansas I watched the weather forecast. I did not care particularly about the forecast for Arkansas. After all, if I wished to know the weather there, all I needed to do was look out my window. I wanted to know if the Cimarron Valley was safe and if the plains to the east were suffering.

I know the storms that sweep in from the north, drop over the Black Mesa, and scour across the Panhandle. They can be swift, and they are merciless. The road runs straight west through the Panhandle, and the norther comes howling in from the side with killer force. The unlucky traveler caught in one of these blizzards can be blinded in an instant. The road whites out and disappears. The storms are dangerous now in an automobile; to the horsebacker, or the man with a team and wagon, they were deadly.

There are tales told of a way for a man to save himself if he is caught on horseback in a killer blizzard. The rider, they say, must shoot his horse, disembowel it, and creep into the belly cavity. He must also be sure the horse falls with its back to the wind. The snow will mound over the dead horse, and horse and snow will provide adequate shelter. There is a danger of the horse freezing solid and entrapping the person inside. On the high plains, it might be days before the horse thawed enough for one to escape; therefore, be warned that it is wise to save the heart and keep it handy for food.

I don't know if this tale is true. I have heard old settlers swear to it, but it never happened to them personally, always to someone who died long ago or else left the country. I don't know if a full-grown man would even fit into the belly of a horse. I imagine that this tale is just another one told to impress the tenderfoot.

Oh, I just flat don't believe any of this story. If it were so, then at one time or another it would have happened that a horse with its freezing rider aboard would have drifted before the storm into some isolated area. There the rider would have performed his desperate ritual, crept inside the horse, and frozen to death. In the spring, after the buzzards and the ants, it would have happened that a cowboy hunting strays would have chanced across the skeleton of a horse with the skeleton of a man tucked neatly inside, and I think we all would have heard of that, and I never did, not once.

I have recently read in the *Reader's Digest* of two men who actually did kill their horse and disembowel it. They were able to warm themselves over the steaming entrails, and then, taking turns, shelter themselves in the body cavity of the horse. From the graphic description in the *Digest*, freezing to death seems almost preferable.

Jiggs Collins was caught in a storm on Christmas Eve, coming down a canyon on an icy road. His pickup skidded and slid off an embankment into the creek below. Jiggs told it like this:

> There I was with my pickup on its left side; my left arm was outside the pickup and pinned against the ground by the cab. I reached up behind my head and got my gun. All the tendons in the back of my right hand had been cut and the blood was pouring. I tried to get my gun under the cab to pry it up so I could get my arm out, but I just couldn't. The gun was slippery with blood, and I had no strength at all in my hand because of the cut tendons. It was getting dark, and colder by the second. I looked at my hunting knife dangling from the dashboard and wondered if I had the guts to cut off my arm to free myself. The very thought shot such a thrill of fear through me that I just grabbed that rifle, stuck it through the window, and raised that whole truck about a foot.

Jiggs stumbled down the canyon to a phone and called his brother Bob in Boise City. Bob and a friend who owned an airplane flew up from Boise City and got Jiggs back to a doctor.

We didn't have tornados in the Valley, but my mother was convinced that one would happen eventually. She had been brought up in the middle of Tornado Alley, that giant swath of land extending through America's midsection from the Gulf to Michigan. She always felt the lack of a storm cellar. I was glad we didn't have one, because she would have made us spend every storm inside it.

Mother tried not to transmit her terror of storms to her five children, but she imposed strange little rituals on us. During a heavy thunderstorm she would make us stay in separate rooms, reasoning, I presume, that even if our house were destroyed perhaps some of her children would survive if they were scattered around. She wouldn't let us go to the bathroom, either. She felt—and for all I know she was right—that a lightning bolt striking anywhere within a mile would travel through the ground, into the plumbing, and up a stream of water, and would electrocute anyone rash enough to be on the toilet. I have managed to overcome my fear to some extent, but I still prefer not to pee during a storm. Sandy, my oldest child, was completely converted. She will not let anyone near the bathroom when lightning is flashing.

Several years after Jiggs Collins and I were divorced I married Walter Hanners. We leased the Goodson Ranch from Mother and moved there with my three oldest children, Sandy, Jeanne, and Kelly. We had been living there for over a year when we had our own experience with the treacherous weather of the Cimarron. In the high country, in the thin, dry air, the temperature can drop with appalling swiftness. My family and I were at the schoolhouse, where I was serving as an official for the school-board election. The weather was clear and fairly temperate for February, so when the teacher asked us to stay for dinner and cards, we accepted. When we went out to leave, the temperature was below freezing, but it didn't seem so bad. We were only about two and a half miles from home. We had gone a mile or a little more when I realized the temperature had fallen alarmingly. Even with the heater on, our breath was frosting the inside of the car windows.

Suddenly the car stopped. Unable to see because of the frosted windows, Walter had missed a turnout and had stuck the car in half-frozen mud.

We should have started walking immediately, but Walter was desperately trying to free the car. In five minutes we were chilled to the bone, and the mud was freezing around the tires. Finally Walter knew we had to walk. He put Jeanne and Sandy on either side of me and draped a blanket around our shoulders. "Now, walk steadily," he directed us, "and don't try to run or even hurry. I'll come behind and carry Kelly."

We started off. The wind was almost at our backs and the blanket helped. We made fairly good time until we got to the gate and the road turned sharply right. The wind whipped the blanket from our shoulders. We could see the house in the distance, a dark mass against the snow.

I was leading Jeanne by the hand, and we were both stumbling and falling. The snow crust would not support our weight, and we were stepping through the crust into deep snow. The road was only two tracks through the snow, and I could not keep hold of Jeanne's hand and stay in the track.

Freezing destroys reasoning power. It seemed to me that I simply was not going to make it. I was five months pregnant with Susan, and was exhausted. I told Sandy to go on ahead to the house as quickly as she could. I think I thought Walter would surely save Jeanne and Kelly, and if Sandy could get to the house all my children would make it through the ordeal. I looked back and saw Walter and Kelly walking along a hundred yards or so behind us. Kelly was tripping lightly along on top of the snow crust. He was nearly four, but he weighed only thirty-two pounds.

I wanted to quit, but Jeanne was tugging at my hand, so we walked on. We came up the last little slope to the house, and I could see Sandy standing in the door. She had been unable to turn the doorknob with her numbed fingers.

I fumbled the door open and pushed the girls into the house and on into the bedroom. We were all three crying from the pain in our hands and feet. I put the girls in bed and covered them deep with blankets.

When I got back to the kitchen, Walter and Kelly were coming through the door. We put Kelly into the bed with the girls and got a fire started. Then I became hysterical. I was cramping and vomiting, and I was afraid I would miscarry. My feet were full of cactus spines, and my toes and fingers were severely frostbitten. I was in worse shape than the others because, as an official at the election, I had worn a dress. They, at least, had on warm jeans. All of us had frostbitten fingers and toes, and Jeanne's double chin was badly frostbitten.

We survived, but not everyone was that lucky. Two cowmen were also caught out that bitter, bitter night. George Wiley was horseback. From the tracks in the snow, it seems that the horse bolted when George got off to open the gate. George began to hike home but didn't make it. He fell close by the road and died there. Ben Brown came driving along, and his car stalled out. Ben got out of his car and walked home. When George Wiley's body was found, it was so close to Ben's car that everyone assumed it was Ben. Ben's boys went out to the ranch to take care of the stock and were shocked when Ben walked out of the bedroom. Then, of course, George Wiley was identified.

It was nineteen degrees below zero that night, and a high wind was blowing. I don't know how high the wind was because we had no weather report. We didn't know about chill factors then. We just knew that it was much harder to survive if the wind was blowing.

Our fingers and toes peeled and cracked and bled. I recently asked Sandy about her memory of that night, and she remembered that I had told Jeanne and her not to cry because their lashes could freeze together. Sandy also remembered throwing away her steel-rimmed glasses. They were freezing to her face, and she tore them off and dropped them to the ground. We walked back down the road after a thaw, and there the glasses were. They had been run over, but were only bent a little.

I began writing stories for *The New Mexico Stockman* in the early '50s. I wrote for it, off and on, for the next decade and gradually gained a minor fame for my stories of the West. Every now and then someone would tell me a story of a noteworthy person or event. One such remarkable man was Charley Wire; here is my poem about him.

Charley Wire

Charley Wire and his two sidekicks
riding from Clayton to the Point of Rocks
were caught in a blizzard,
in a web of wind and slashing snow.

Charley Wire called to his pardners,
kept on calling when they didn't answer,
left his horse when it fell down dead.
Walked on and on through the wild white darkness

twenty miles to a sheepherder's camp.
His feet fell off in bits and pieces.
Some men refuse to die.

I don't know how he did it. I was ready to give up after a quarter of a mile when our hands and feet were only a little frostbitten. Charley Wire's feet were frozen, and of course were destroyed. It is incredible that he lived, but he did. He rode with his crutches strapped to the side of his saddle, just above his gun scabbard.

I remember a hailstorm that frightened me almost as much as our trek through the subzero weather. The sky had been overcast all day, and it was quite warm. I left my four children and went to bring in the cows for the evening milking. I was about a quarter mile from the house when the sky changed.

It changed in an instant from placid gray to a roiling, angry purple and green. I ran; I had to get back to the house before the storm hit. Sandy had already lit the kerosene lamp when I got into the house just ahead of the storm. It had seemed to me as I ran that the worst of the storm was coming from the southwest, so I put the children on the old sofa against the north wall. We cowered there listening to the roar of the approaching hail. A hailstone the size of a golf ball crashed through the north window at our right, shattering glass over us. I screamed, "Sandy, get Susie." I grabbed Jeanne and Kelly by the hands, and we went through flying glass to the middle bedroom, where we flung ourselves on the floor at the foot of the bed. I snatched the quilts off the bed and threw them over our heads, in case the storm changed direction. Then I thought of the kerosene lamp we had left sitting on the table near the windows. Too near the windows. I had to get it. I could see our home burning on the inside while the hail tore at it from the outside.

I said, "Sandy, no matter what, you keep the little kids right here until I get back. I'm going after the lamp."

I slid out from under the quilts, went through the bedroom on the east, and looked into the room we had just fled. The storm had gotten stronger, and hail and shards of glass were flying across the room. The lamp stood there fifteen feet away, miraculously untouched. I shielded my eyes with my arm and stepped out into that destruction. I could feel glass biting into my arm and shoulder, but I reached the lamp and picked it up to light my way back to safety. There were eight panes of glass, two feet square, on the north side of that room, and the hail was coming through them with such force that each stone was drilling through the pane, taking with it shards and splinters of glass.

That was a long fifteen feet back. I held the lamp with both hands, shielding it with my body. I slowly shuffled through glass and hailstones to the south bedrooms. I set the lamp on a dresser, blew it out, and crawled back under the quilts with the children. I could feel blood trickling down my back, but I was reasonably sure there were no major cuts. We crouched under those quilts for nearly an hour before the horrible noise finally subsided. When the sound of crashing glass and hail changed to the drumming of rain, I threw off the quilts and lit the lamp. I saw Sandy's face turn pale, and she said, so quietly that I knew she was trying not to frighten the younger children, "Mama, you've got a little blood on your arm. You better let me get it off." She took the lamp and went into the kitchen and returned with a wet towel. As she sponged off the blood and picked little pieces of glass out of my arms, shoulders, and back, she whispered, "Mama, there's not a pane of glass left in the kitchen, and there's hail and water all over the floor, and the little kids haven't had any supper."

"Okay, kids," I said, "The storm's over now, and we're going to have a picnic right here. Sandy, you spread a sheet on the floor, and I'll go get the food." I went to the kitchen and took bread, cold fried venison, pickles, jam, and butter from the cupboard.

Jeanne, who was eight then, Kelly, my son, who was six, and Susan, who was just past a year, were known as the little kids, in contrast to Sandy, only twelve then, but already taller than I. She was my big girl, and I know I put too much on her. She was my second lieutenant, the next in command at home. Sandy took responsibility for the younger children, helped with the cooking, the laundry, and that endless ironing with those horrible sadirons heated on the woodburning stove. She delegated labor to the younger children, sending one to gather eggs and another to get in wood. She changed the baby.

The night of the storm, after we had fed the little kids, I put them all three in one bed and told them that as a special treat I would leave them a lamp and they could look at books as long as they liked. Then Sandy and I went in to survey the wreckage.

All the windows in both the kitchen and living room were gone. The screens that were supposed to protect the windows hung in tatters. The rain had stopped, but a north wind blew across the piles of hail, and it was very cold. I swept the glass from the window seats, and Sandy and I nailed comforters over the windows. I built up the fire, noticing as I swept the stove that I was going to have to throw away a fresh pot of beans. The lid was so thickly covered by glass, it would be impossible to lift without glass falling into the food.

Sandy dumped the wood from the washboiler we used for a woodbox, and we began cleaning. I was frantic to get the water off the floors before the boards warped and ruined. We picked up and swept up the glass and swept the water out of doors. Hail was banked solidly against both the east and west doors, and in the dim lamplight I could see drifts of hail two feet high in the yard.

We went to bed about three, but I couldn't sleep. I knew all the grass would be gone, ground down under the hail, and I was afraid we had lost stock. I didn't see how anything could have survived that merciless pounding. I was worried, too, about my husband Walter, who had gone into Boise City on a business trip. I had told the kids, "Now your dad won't be in tonight. He's got more sense than to start out in a storm like this." But still I was worried. I was up at daybreak, and as I walked from room to room, all I could see out the doors and windows was destruction. The trees were stripped bare, and my flowers and late garden lay under drifts of ice. I could see ground under the hail where the grass had been beaten away. It was the ninth of September, and I knew there wouldn't be enough warm weather for the grass to come back. I looked to the east and saw three dead animals, and knew the milk cows and a saddle horse were gone.

As I looked northeast, I saw the old blue pickup come creeping around the end of the Mesa. It was Walter, driving as fast as the mud and ice would let him. I called to Sandy to bring the children, and we all stepped outside to meet him. I wanted him to see that at least his family was alive.

He said he had driven as far as he could, and had stayed at a farmhouse along the way. The storm had reached Boise City and beyond, hitting in strips. Kenton had been skipped over, the storm hitting again at the 101 Hill.

North, all we could see were the piles of ice. Walter and I started walking past the barn to the southwest. We reached the end of the hail twenty yards behind our barn. It looked as if a mowing machine had gone along, cutting a swath. The entire ranch and our small herd of cattle had been spared with the exception of the northeast half-section where the house was.

The cloud I had seen coming from the southwest had wiped out our neighbor there. The cloud that wrecked our house had come from the north. No two people who lived through that storm could ever agree on its direction. From what I saw of the sky before it hit, it seemed that there were several storms racing in different directions, and that must have been the way of it.

The people of the Cimarron can find something to laugh about even in a tragic storm. The prized story of the big hail concerned Frank Behimer and his thumbs. Frank saw the storm coming even as I did. He guessed correctly that his big plate-glass window was in jeopardy. He was determined not to lose that window, so he and his wife ran and got an enormous sheet of tin. Frank leaned it against the window, got between the window and the tin, and hooked his thumbs over the side edge of the tin to steady it. He stood there for forty-five minutes, unable to move or change positions, while the hail beat his thumbs flat. He couldn't just let go for fear the force of the storm would blow away the tin and endanger even more mortal areas of his body. Forty-five minutes of intense storm is a mighty long time, and my children and I under our quilt, and Frank under his sheet of tin, thought that surely it would be over any minute. It seemed a hellish long time to me, but to Frank, whose thumbs were being maimed, it must have seemed forever. Poor Frank was sheepish about the whole episode. It must have been a real pain to explain over and over that he was wearing bandages because his thumbs had been broken in a hailstorm.

A strange thing happened after that storm. The country that had been hit burst into bloom. The leaves had been stripped from the trees and shrubs, and ice had packed around them, chilling the roots. The plants evidently thought that winter had come and gone and it was spring again. For a few days at the last of September, the plum thickets bloomed, the trees put forth new little leaves, and the lilac bush in the front yard bloomed again. Then the killing frosts came, and fall and winter were again with us.

Brief Winter

> The storm crashed down
> and scythed the land
> with wrack and rain
> and hail as large as orient pearl.
> A brief hard winter savaged there
> and reft that land of all it bore.
> The earth, that tired old trull,
> was tricked
> by patterns true in other springs.

Girl on a Pony

She primped some bloom
on dry dull boughs,
greened her limbs,
and waited then,
till winter broke that spell.

Chapter 2

The Women

My mother, born Stella Ellis, was a teacher. She was born in Yell County, Arkansas. After her father died in the great typhoid epidemic in the late 1800s, my grandmother remarried and brought her family to Devol, Oklahoma.

Mother went to college. She walked out of the cotton field with the pitifully small amount of money a tiny woman could make picking cotton. She took the examination for a teacher's certificate and began teaching when she was eighteen. I do not know where in Oklahoma she taught, but it was in a one-room school with eight grades. She taught one year; then she and her brother Sam went away to college in Weatherford. They got a tiny two-room apartment and put a cot in the kitchen for Sam. Mother had the other little room. This was in 1912.

They had no money, but Mother clerked in a dime store on Saturday for one dollar, and that dollar bought food for the week. On Sunday she cooked an enormous pot of butter beans, and when the beans were done, she dumped in a package of elbow macaroni. That was their food until the next Sunday. Once during the year, her mother sent a ham from the farm they were sharecropping. Mother and Sam cherished every bite of that ham, finally using the bone to season a pot of beans.

I suppose the real miracle was that these two children of sharecroppers made it out to college at all. Their older brother, Roscoe, had gone to the university, how or when I do not know. I do know that not one step of those three Ellises' way to education was easy—no scholarships, no work-study, and no educational grants. Just hard work and grinding poverty.

After that one year away at college, Mother went back to teaching in Oklahoma. It doesn't matter where. I know what the school was like. It was like Cora's school, and the school I went to in the Cimarron Valley. There was one big room with the blackboard on the end behind the teacher's desk. A map case was on a wall, and brown pictures of Abraham Lincoln and George Washington. There was a flag, I'm sure. A big coal or wood stove stood in the middle of the room, roasting the children next to it while those on the outskirts froze. A water bucket with a dipper stood against the wall near the door. There was an organ in Cora's school, but there was no such wealth in my school, nor I expect in those where Mother taught.

There couldn't have been much difference in the children. In the photograph of Cora's pupils the boys stand there looking pale and perhaps too thin in their bib overalls and heavy shoes. The girls are suspiciously well dressed, as if they might have had some advance notice

Cora Wince and students. (Center for Southwest Research, General Library, University of New Mexico, 992-018)

of the picture taking, and I suspect Cora brought the piece of fancywork from home to display it on the corner of her desk. Her work is unfinished, the embroidery hoop still on the piece. I believe it is appliqué work, but it could be solid embroidery. Women did such things then. They worked endless hours to create one scarf or tablecloth. They needed these little bits of beauty. There is not much else of beauty in the photograph except, of course, Cora's watch.

When my brother Felix was taken prisoner by the Japanese in 1941, Mother began a piece of fancywork. She bleached out a fifty-pound sugar sack and, although some of the blue lettering was still on the sack, started a border of drawnwork around it. I was amazed. I had never seen such work, and had no idea that my mother could do such complicated, intricate lace. I just went in and got the little cloth out of the cedar chest to study it. The blue lettering has long ago faded out, and the cloth is still in perfect condition. To make the lace border, Mother drew out two inches of the warp threads. Then with a needle and linen thread she wove an intricate pattern of lace in the remaining woof threads of the cloth. I was appalled that Mother had started such a tedious piece of work on such poor material. I said, "My god, Mother, you are putting all that work on an old sugar sack. I would have bought you the finest linen."

Mother smoothed the work over her knee and said, "Oh, no, this is good enough." She was right. Sugar sacks in those days were made of good strong cotton cloth. It is still whole after fifty years. She finished it just before Felix came home in 1945.

I grew up watching Mother tat. Tatting is surely the slowest and most difficult of all lace making, as I learned

Mrs. Fish at exterior and interior of claim shack. The picture of the exterior with its bleak surroundings, contrasted with the cozy interior, symbolizes the lives of women on the homesteads. (Center for Southwest Research, General Library, University of New Mexico, 992-018)

when Mother devoted an entire summer trying to teach me how to tat. Mother was in her seventies then, but her hands were still agile and, to her death at eighty-five, miraculously untouched by arthritis. I watched the tatting shuttle flying between and among her fingers and the fine lace slowly lengthening, then snarled my thread again, cut the knot off, and grimly started over. By the end of the summer I had learned to make the simplest of all tatting patterns, but it was uneven and lumpy.

As Mother tatted and I tried, she told me another incident of that first year she and her brother Sam had gone to college. They had managed tuition and they had Mother's Saturday dollar for food and thought they were doing fine, until Mother found she had to pay a lab fee of one dollar for her Domestic Science course. She had no money at all, so she bravely went to her teacher. The teacher said, "Miss Ellis, don't worry. We can work something out. You can tat, and I need ten yards of tatting for some curtains. I'll pay your lab fee for you, if you will do ten yards of tatting for me." Mother agreed at once.

I looked at the snarled knots and pieces of tatting I had discarded and nearly wept. I still can hardly bear to think of that poor young woman tatting night after night for one dollar. "Mother," I said, "that was criminal. It must have taken forever. Ten yards of tatting for just a dollar."

Mother said, "Oh no, it wasn't so bad. I would come home and eat; then I would go to bed and study my lessons. When I finished studying, I picked up the tatting shuttle and did half a yard, so it only took twenty nights."

Sandy and I came through Weatherford on December 27, 1983, just after the great Christmas storm. For years I have had in my mind a picture of Mother sitting up in bed tatting, but I never thought to ask why she studied and did that lacework in bed. I know the reason now. She was cold. Of course she was cold. How could she not be cold in Weatherford in the winter?

I think we all have fantasies about going back into the past to correct some grievous error or right some wrong. If I could go back in time, I'd go to Weatherford and I would somehow see that my mother got that dollar. That one dollar will haunt me always.

The handwork displayed so carefully on Cora's desk, the drawnwork on my mother's sugar sack, and the bits and pieces of other women's lives I find in the bins at the Salvation Army break my heart. They make me question my own emotions about the Cimarron, the Panhandle, and the life in this most isolated of places. I am constantly homesick for that country, and yet I fled from it. I am driven to return year after year—but then there is the panic that hits me when I go back to Kenton and forces me to flee again.

I am afraid, against all reason, that I will be trapped back there in a time that doesn't even exist now, but that existed for Cora, and for me, and for all the other women who ever pieced a quilt or embroidered a dresser scarf or crocheted a rag rug by the light of a kerosene lamp. I am afraid I will be again trapped in a loneliness so acute that only repetitious movements of the hands can lighten it.

I have a cadre of instant experts on life on the Cimarron—my five children. From time to time I call them and ask them questions. I was thinking of the fancywork that we all did, Cora and my mother and all the other women. I called Susan and asked her why we occupied our time this way. She said, "Why, Mama, that's easy. It's just like Hadley."

I remembered Hadley, a severely retarded man who lived far back up a canyon with his parents. He spent all his days sitting in the sun unraveling gunny sacks. He pulled out the threads one by one and placed them in a pile.

Susan explained. "When I was going to school in the Valley and we saw another person doing something repetitious or meaningless, we always said, 'You're acting like Hadley.' I get compulsive about my handwork, and all the time I'm stitching or sewing I constantly think about that poor man."

It is the loneliness and, of course, the desire to create something beautiful, but more than all else, I believe women's fancywork reflects the desire to turn off the mind. Susan has a hard job. She does something official with the poor and disadvantaged in Monroe County, Michigan. During these years of automobile factory closings and layoffs her job sends her home sick at heart over some crisis she could not avert or some calamity she could not prevent. She tends to her family, and then picks up her stitchery and turns her mind off for a while. That is what my mother was doing when she put drawnwork all around a sugar sack. She didn't have to think about an eighteen-year-old son missing in action in the Philippines. Of course the sugar sack was good enough. She wasn't interested in the finished product, only in the doing of it.

Many times the things women made were not beautiful. I have a pillow top that I found in the Goodwill that is of an unsurpassed ugliness. The woman folded little triangles of thin nylon cloth, laid them in an overlapping pattern, and sewed them to a cotton back. It looks like a square from the back of a particularly repulsive reptile. It isn't even finished. The woman who hand-stitched all those little triangles never even tried to make a pillow. She just made the top and put it aside, and someone threw it away. I hope it served its purpose. I hope the woman who made the pillow top was able to turn her thoughts away from whatever loneliness or fear beset her and gain some sort of peace as she manipulated the little poorly stitched triangles.

I have other things I rescued from the Goodwill: two bunches of grapes (purple thread crocheted around bottle tops), linens, and an old slatted sunbonnet. I wrote a poem about the things I've found in thrift stores.

Mining Junk

I mine old junk,
searching through the scree
of mountains of old clothes
and cardboard boxes
for the things that some dead mother's daughter
threw away.

They sift out.

The coat of black brocade,
handwoven silk,
the son brought home
in 1945.

Linen handkerchiefs
a breath would float away,
and tablecloth and napkins
from the torn down looms of Ireland.

A handspun coverlet,
double woven, black on blue
from some Ozark mountain cabin
where a woman sat by lamplight
flashing shuttles back and forth.

I tunnelled through a bin of toys
and found a mother lode of cloisonne,
a box from China,
a belt buckle,
a little silver horse.

I saw a trace of color
in a biscuit tin of buttons
and panned an opal out.

I take these treasures home
and salt my house
with riches for my daughters so that they
can throw their own dead mother's things away.

The slatted sunbonnet hangs by my door, as I saw my
mother's bonnets hang by the ranch-house door. Mine is
red calico with the original heavy cardboard staves.
When I found that bonnet I remembered vividly a small
tableau: two women standing isolated in the middle of
the garden, with their sunbonnets on.

Men went outside after company dinners and sat on
the running boards of cars or leaned against a corral gate
to talk. Women went to the middle of their gardens. There
they were safe and could talk about private things. I went
to see a friend once, and she said to me, "You haven't
seen my plants." She took me out back to the patio, and
we talked there. She told me about a very dark side of her
life. The image of two women talking in a garden stayed
with me for years.

Gardens

Women went to gardens then,
secure terrain
from husbands who would never go
and children who were forbidden.
They talked, their faces hidden
in the slatted caves of calico.

They spoke of pain
and pregnancy and blood,
the ceaseless work,
children daft from birth,
the men.

We still go there,
on this paved earth,
to tiny gardens hung on knotted strings.
We stand and stare into Boston fern
and tell each other dreadful things.

Once during the bad drought of the fifties I crocheted a

rag rug. I collected rags, cut them into strips, and sewed the strips together. I sat there night after night in my old blue rocking chair and doggedly thrust that whittled cedar hook through the edge of the rug, pulling a loop through and gaining yet another stitch. I hadn't done very many rows when I realized the rug wasn't going to be a success, but I didn't stop. While I was working on the rug, I didn't have to think of the lack of rain, the hungry cattle, and the worry that, in spite of all my canning, there wasn't much food left in the house and there was no money to buy more. I put the rug aside only when I was so tired that I knew I could sleep.

When the rug was finished, I spread it on the floor. It was ugly and misshapen, with a big hump in the middle. As I looked, I thought no woman should be so desperate that she would crochet a rag rug four feet in diameter. I walked toward the kitchen, and as I passed by the shelves in the hall, a cloud of depression and despair enveloped me. It was a tangible thing, a weight so heavy I grabbed the edge of a shelf to support myself, and I thought, "Somehow I will get out of this. Somehow I will escape."

For many years I had been writing—not much, and with no idea of "sending it off." I just wrote stuff down. I wrote to *The New Mexico Stockman* and asked them if they would like to see some humorous articles on the West. They said they would. I sent them a short article, and they sent me a check for twenty dollars. I took that twenty dollars and my five children, and I escaped from the Valley. I went back to school.

Years after, I taught a poetry workshop in the Women's Unit of the Arkansas Department of Corrections. One of my best poets, Gloria, was paroled and got a job at a garment factory there in Pine Bluff. She lived two blocks from me, and one night she walked over. "When I was in prison," she said, "I got up, ate breakfast, and went to work sewing. Then I ate my supper and went to bed, almost too tired to sleep. Now I get up, eat, and go to work sewing. I come home, eat, and go to bed. So tell me, what's the difference?"

I wanted to cry, because I could not help her. I could not tell her of the prisons we all find ourselves in, but I did write a poem for Gloria and for all the women in the Arkansas prison.

A Lecture for the Women's Unit
at the Arkansas Department of Correction

See this picture, ladies,
the miles of desert
sun, and sand.
The long thin line of trees
that follows down
the meager river.
The mesa like a black wall
to the north.
(On the other side lies Denver.)

A spacious prison, ladies.
I could see
to the north, five miles,
and to the south, the same.
To the east and west
the canyon stretched
for forty miles and more.

In my private cell
some thirteen trees
grew beside a spring that trickled up through clay
to bring
bitter water to that thirsty land.

A captured coyote walks his cage,
an endless circling pace
from side to side.
I walked
west to the thirteen trees
north to the barbed wire fence
and to the south and east the same.

I came
at last to peace.
I thought to write
and sent these bits and pieces
out beyond the wire.
Each day I did not kill myself
until the mail had run.

A rain, a poem, a flood—
who knows?
But I walked west one day
and found the spring
beneath the thirteen trees
had broken loose.
The ground was wet
and all the wires were down.

Mother became the owner of a dried-out ranch and a

herd of starving cattle in 1936 when my father died. She never learned to ride a horse, so she walked her ranch. She knew her cattle almost individually, and kept careful watch over the young heifers that were about to calve. It was not at all unusual to look out and see Mother slowly herding two or three cows before her to the house-pasture gate. These were range cattle, and not at all tame. Mother must have just slowly and gently shooed the cows along, flapping her sunbonnet and apron. That sunbonnet saved her life on one of her weekly journeys.

A week before, Patches, an unbroken little black and white pinto mare, had foaled, but the colt was unable to get to its feet. Jiggs and I were at the ranch, and Jiggs went out and carried the little colt to the barn. Jiggs put a halter on Patches's head, and he and Mother tried to hold the colt up so it could nurse. They worked with the colt for hours, but it had been born prematurely and had no strength. After it died, Jiggs took Patches back to the big pasture.

Mother went out on her weekly trip around the place. Patches saw her and trotted up to her. Mother patted her on the nose and said, "Poor Patches, you lost your baby." Patches sniffed at Mother's coat and then trotted off. Mother was continuing her walk when she heard hooves pounding toward her. She looked around and saw Patches coming toward her at a run. The mare's ears were laid back and her teeth were bared. Mother snatched off her bonnet and held it by the strings. As Patches reared to strike with her front feet, Mother hit her in the face with the sunbonnet. Patches retreated, then whirled to attack again. Mother hit her again with the bonnet and then ran. Mother was only twenty or so yards from a fence, and she

fought that crazed mare every step. She reached the
fence, and with one last yell and one more slash with her
bonnet, drove Patches back a few feet. Mother dropped to
the ground and rolled under the fence.

I was at the ranch when Mother came in. She sank
into a chair and turned toward me a face so ashen and
strained that I thought she had been snake bit and was
dying.

Mother told me what had happened, then said,
"Patches thought I had done away with her baby. I had on
this same coat when we were working with the colt, and
she caught its scent. She's not vicious, just crazy with
grief."

Truly, Patches was not vicious. She was one of the
horses Jiggs and I broke when we were in our horse-
breaking and training careers.

We actually made a little money at that endeavor,
which is not surprising, all things considered. Jiggs
brought the raw broncs down from on top, *on top* being
the generic location which meant any place outside of the
Valley. He rode them first to see if they were going to
buck. I rode them next.

Jiggs eared the horse down. (*Earing down* means to
grab a horse's ear and twist it.) Any horse will stand as
still as death if someone has twisted an ear and is holding
on to it. It doesn't hurt the horse, but it does make him
very, very angry. As soon as Jiggs got a horse eared down,
I got on the horse and took a very tight grip on the reins.
When I was securely in the saddle, Jiggs turned loose of
the ear and jumped back. The horse inevitably bolted, for
which I was always grateful. A bolting horse I could ride,
superb horsewoman that I was. A bucking horse would

have flung me to glory. After the horse bolted all he
wanted to (I certainly couldn't do anything to stop him) I
would turn his head back toward the corrals, where Jiggs
had thoughtfully positioned a row of barrels. I neck-
reined the horse back and forth around the barrels. Jiggs
and I trained some good saddle horses. I remember some
of them: a pair of big gray horses named (with great
ingenuity) Silver and Blue, Patches, of course, a sorrel
mare named Satin, and Trinkalo and Buck.

Even as I write this, I can hardly believe I let that
maniac cowboy put me up on untrained horses. I have a
vivid picture of myself hunched over the saddle horn, hair
snapping in the wind, while Silver or Blue or Buck ran
wildly across the flat, completely out of control.

Jiggs and I had been divorced for many years when
we met again in Santa Fe for Jeanne's wedding. We were
sitting at a table drinking coffee when I happened to think
of our horse-training episode. I said, "Jiggs, do you remember when we used to break horses for a living?"

"Sure, I remember."

"Jiggs, tell me something then. Were you stealing
those horses?"

Jiggs groaned at my stupidity. "Well of course I was
stealing those horses. Where did you think I got them?
You knew we didn't have any money."

That was certainly true. We were incredibly poor. We
quit the horse-training venture, and Jiggs went to ride for
George Wiggins. I think we stopped breaking horses
because I was into my third pregnancy.

Jiggs's cousin, Glenn Capansky, had been farming
where we were living, and we took over from him. Glenn
and Sylvia had planted a huge garden and had a small

herd of milk cows. I was there alone with two small
children and heavy with pregnancy. I milked five cows
morning and night, ran the separator, and put the cream
into cans for Jiggs to take every Monday morning to the
mailbox. We didn't have a car, of course, and Jiggs had
rigged a small platform on the back of the Ford tractor to
carry the five-gallon cans of cream.

Years later, when I was teaching at the University of
Arkansas, a student wrote a sentence that brought back a
vivid memory of those cream cans. The following poem
was published in the Ball State University Forum and also
included in the book *Westering*.

Can of Sad

"It make me fill can of sad,"
my student wrote.
And I reading, red pencil ready
fell straight into that metaphor.

My junkyard life was filled with cans
all spilling sad.

We carried lunch to school in cans
that once held Armour's lard,
or Karo syrup.
Those lids, pried up with rusty nails,
set free a thick dark smell
of sardines, peanut butter,
and soggy homemade bread.
I don't like oranges either.

The county agent came one spring.
My father killed a cow
And all the ladies came
to cut and pack the meat
in tin this time
instead of the old familiar Mason jars.

Those cans blew up all summer.
Sometimes in Mother's face
or in our hands
as we ran a race to throw
a bulging can
into the big arroyo.

We loved that summer.
It livened up our days
to see our winter's food
go off like rockets.

The cream cans.
I was dead poor and grown
before I knew about
five-gallon cans of sour cream
shipped by mail to Santa Fe.

Cream checks bought shoes and sugar.

The cat fell in.
I fished him out
and scraped him with a cedar chip.
If you think I threw that cream away
you're wrong.

You have to be dead poor to know
I'd have wrung out a rattlesnake
to save that cream.

My student's metaphor extended far
beyond all reason.
I laid aside
the essay and my pen and hammered down
the lids on all those cans.

How Mother got to Colorado I never thought to ask, but she met and married my dad there. She was clerking in a department store in Pueblo when Dad came in to buy a pair of shoes. My parents made a strange couple. Dad was six feet four and Mother was barely five feet tall. Felix Goodson was flamboyant, always striving for attention, and getting it. He was a master politician, a wonderful jokester and teller of tales. Stella Goodson was almost pathologically unassuming. In her eyes, the worst sins were showing off and bragging. So, of course, she had to marry a man who was a monumental showoff.

Dad had been a wanderer, playing first base for a minor-league ball club in Texas, catching red-hot rivets in steel structures, or working as a butcher. My grandfather, Milton Goodson, was a butcher in Anniston, Alabama. When my dad was in the third grade, my grandfather took him out of school to deliver meat on the streets of Anniston. Milton Goodson reckoned that third grade was enough education for anyone.

Dad had taught himself to read very well, and he could sign his name. He could handle math, but he had never learned, or had forgotten, how to write. He couldn't even make all the letters. Mother wrote all Dad's letters for him, and that was a great humiliation to him. He was truly jealous of Mother's education. He felt that if he had even graduated from the eighth grade, he would have been unstoppable. He loved the political struggle, even though his highest office was that of county commissioner.

Dad was a yellow-dog Democrat, and Franklin D. Roosevelt was his idol. One of Dad's greatest moments came when he met Roosevelt in Trinidad, Colorado. Dad had driven a hundred miles to see Roosevelt as he passed through on a whistle-stop campaign. Dad was so impressed by his meeting with Roosevelt that he copied his act.

Dad went to Chicago with a trainload of cattle. Every time the train stopped along the journey, Dad hung out of the caboose and made an impassioned speech for the election of F.D.R. Sometimes his only audience was a bemused brakeman, but sometimes he had a crowd of twenty or thirty.

When she met Dad, Mother had already filed on a homestead in Colorado, six hundred and forty acres, eighteen miles east of Trinidad. After they were married, Mother and Dad loaded a wagon with building materials and housekeeping goods and creaked out to the claim. Mother made a small camp while Dad dug the excavation for the half-dugout.

It almost seems to me that I can remember this little claim shack where I was born, but perhaps I have heard Mother describe it so often that I feel I remember it. The one room was small, twelve by twelve, I believe. The floor at first was dirt. Mother dampened it and pounded it, time

LaVerne and John Goodson by the claim-shack wall, 1923. (Photo by Stella Goodson, Collection of LaVerne Hanners)

and time again, until it became almost as hard and slick as glass.

The board walls of the house protruded about three feet above the prairie. It must have been the most lonely-looking home in the world—miles and miles of sweeping prairie, no trees, nothing but a few mesquite bushes and cactus, and then suddenly this little half- house sticking up three feet above the grass, with a plume of smoke rising from the stovepipe in the corner.

Four steps were cut into the wall, leading up to the surface. There was a door at the bottom of the steps. In the summer a cretonne curtain hung in the doorway, letting in air and light. The claim shack had windows right under the tin roof. These windows, too, were cur-tained with cretonne. I don't suppose many people are still left who remember cretonne.

Cretonne

Cretonne was the poor folks' fabric,
sometimes on sale for seven cents a yard.
A dollar bought enough to put
curtains at a claim shack window
or to hang across the dugout door
at the bottom of the steps.

The cloth was bright
with huge unlikely flowers,
pink roses big as pumpkins,
lilies, leaves and vines
and every manner
of lovely, lavish color.

Eyes seek color on the Colorado flats.
The cretonne was a treasure.
We could stare until our eyes
could accept again
the endless sweep of dead prairie grass.

At night we looked at cretonne
here and there about the one-room shack,
table runners, pillow tops, the curtains.
In the golden haze of lamplight
the cretonne bloomed.
Flowers flowed and shifted in the light.
Soft muted pinks and blues,
lavender and vining green
all came alive.

The cretonne tuned our eyes to color
and printed some motifs upon our brains:
English ivy, fleur-de-lis
and gardens full of cabbage rose.

My older brother was born in Oklahoma at my grand-mother's house, but my younger brother and I were born in the claim shack. I remember when my own children were born—the starched nurses wheeling me into the delivery room; the delivery room itself, brightly lighted, sterile, with white-clad figures bustling around helping me, taking care of me—and then I think of what my own birth must have been like.

I was born July 15, 1921, in the middle of the worst storm that ever hit those flats. Water and hail washed down the dugout walls and swirled around my dad's feet as he held the smoky lamp up so the doctor could see to deliver me. The doctor had splashed through mud and heavy rain all the way from Trinidad in his Model T. Doctors don't have to do *that* any more, and thank God for that. The good old days may have had some charms, but they were certainly hell on women.

We moved from Colorado to New Mexico in 1925, and this I do remember. Dad had a new Model T, so we came along in style. I remember coming through Tollgate Canyon and Dad pointing out the rocks where the tollgate used to be. I remember when we caught up with the wagonload of furniture that had preceded us by two days, and I do well remember my first sight of the Cimarron Valley. The high mesas on either side, the winding river lined with cottonwoods, and the fields of alfalfa enchanted me as they do now.

I have written stories about the delights of growing up in the Cimarron Valley, and truly it was idyllic in those years before the Great Drought. But as I remember back, I wonder if even then it was such a wonderful time for Mother. I never heard her complain, but the work she had to do on a big combination alfalfa and cattle ranch must have been appalling. Mother did not teach school when we children were small, and I'm sure that was because she didn't have time. My two younger sisters, Virginia and Barbara, were born after we came to New Mexico. So Mother had not only the cooking for the family and ranch hands, but also the care of us three older children and the two babies.

I think children seldom really see their parents. I have pictures of my mother in my mind, like stills from a movie film. Mostly these pictures are of Mother doing some-

thing. I cannot call to mind any vision of her in repose. I
doubt if I saw her much just sitting quietly. One vivid
memory I have is of Mother cutting enormous loaves of
bread from a large dishpan of dough. She would lift the
dough partly from the pan and whack off a sizable chunk
with a long and wicked-looking butcher knife. I remember her wringing the necks of a half-dozen chickens. I
would have matched Mother against all comers for short-
est time in getting a chicken from the chicken yard to the
table.

I remember Mother bending over the scrubboard,
before my dad bought her the first washing machine to
come to the Valley. It was a Maytag, one of those old
brutes with a gasoline motor and a pedal that one had to
stomp to start. Women came from miles around to see
that machine. It wasn't long before every rancher's wife
in the Valley had one. The favorite make was a Maytag,
mostly because of the wringer. It had big soft rollers that
were much safer than the small, hard rubber rollers on
the wringers of other makes. I believe the big roller was
one of the selling points of the Maytag machine. The
salesman started the motor, then stuck his hand between
the rollers to demonstrate their safety.

When I think of the chore it was to do the laundry for a
large family, I realize that the advent of the motor-driven
washer must have seemed like the end of slavery.

I watched Mother wash on a washboard. It was just
horrible. In the interest of preserving some of the more
dreadful customs of the old West, here follow the directions for hand laundry, western style, the way my mother
did it. She was not dabbling out a few undies, she was
doing an industrial-sized washing for herself and Dad,

three older children, and a baby or two. Dad wore khaki
pants and shirts around the ranch. The boys wore denim
overalls, the kind with buckled suspenders, and wool
knee pants for dress up. Mother, the little girls, and I all
wore dresses that Mother had made, sewing them up on
the old treadle Singer sewing machine. These clothes,
along with the sheets, pillowcases, dishtowels, towels,
and underwear, were the clothes Mother scrubbed every
week on the board.

First she provided herself with a large amount of
firewood. Then she built a fire under the huge iron washpot, which she had filled with buckets of water from the
vat in the milk house. When the water was hot she threw a
tablespoon of lye into the water to ''break'' it. I am not
sure of the precise chemical reaction involved in this
procedure, but the water was very hard, and the lye
caused the minerals to separate out of the water. A thick
white scum rose to the top of the washpot, and Mother
skimmed it off with an old wooden-handled cooking pot.

After the water was hot Mother dipped out enough to
warm up the water in the washtub. She grabbed a bar of
homemade soap, rubbed it on a garment, and scrubbed
the garment briskly against the corrugated washboard.
She put the white clothes into the pot to boil awhile, but
the colored clothes went directly into the rinse tub. After
rinsing, of course, all the clothes were wrung out by hand
and hung on the line to dry. It took hours and hours, and it
was the most brutal, woman-killing job in the world.

I can remember the washing and I remember the
ironing with those dreadful old sadirons. What I cannot
remember are the clothes themselves. I know most of my
dresses and the little girls' dresses would have been made

of feed sacking, that marvelous 100-percent cotton material that the mills sacked their feeds and flours in. Women
cherished those yards of material, and went with their
husbands to pick out the sacks of feed with matching
designs. I recall our shopping in Kenton for dress materials, but I cannot remember a single print or dress pattern. Mother used newspaper patterns to cut the cloth.
Newspaper patterns were made by holding a piece of
newspaper up to a person and whacking out the sem-
blance of a neckline and little crescents for the sleeves.
Sometimes Mother took a pattern from another piece of
clothing by placing the garment on a newspaper and
cutting away. These patterns were probably better than
nothing. Mother carefully saved the ones that turned out
well. She rolled them up and tied a piece of bias tape
around the roll. I remember watching her lay the pattern
out on the material, holding it in place with table knives.

Mother also made our underwear. I had a photograph
of myself with four inches of black sateen bloomers
hanging out under my dress. The elastic was far too tight
in those bloomer legs, but I remedied that by pulling the
elastic down below my knees.

I suppose it is just as well that I cannot bring to mind
any of my clothes. I must have been the ultimate in tacky,
if not downright hideous.

I remember one dress Mother had before Dad died. It
was plum-colored satin with a bodice of gold brocade.
The jacket was satin, and there was a matching satin and
gold hat. I thought the dress and hat were the most
beautiful things I had ever seen, and they probably were. I
embarrassed Mother over that dress. There was important company at the ranch. Perhaps they were bankers or

buyers of alfalfa seed or cattle. The men had brought their wives along, and they were beautifully dressed. I was determined that they should see my mother had a dress every bit as fine as theirs. I stepped upstairs and got mother's dress. I came back down to the landing and, leaning out, gently waved that dress like a banner.

There was a stifled giggle or two and then Mother said, "LaVerne, why don't you show the ladies the jacket. It's really the nicest part of the dress."

I was elated. "Can I bring down the hat too?" When Mother nodded I went up like a whirlwind and carefully brought down the jacket and hat. The ladies were gracious and made nice comments. I am to this day almost overcome with gratitude that Mother didn't fail me or make me feel small over this childish bit of bragging.

I do recall what happened to that hat. We had made the journey to Muleshoe, Texas, to visit my grandparents, chugging along in the Model A pickup, Mother and Dad and the two little girls in the front and we three older children in the back. It was August, and John and Felix and I had run wild in Granddad's watermelon patch. He had told us we could have all we wanted. We reveled and rioted in watermelon. John would lift a melon as high as his head and drop it on the ground. Then we dug out the heart with our grubby little hands, eating until the juice spurted out the corners of our mouths, and then moving on to another melon.

We started home, and all three of us promptly came down with magnificent cases of diarrhea.

That trip must have been the stuff of nightmares. Dad said he couldn't go three miles before one child or another banged on the back window of the cab, demanding to be let out by the side of the road. It had rained, and the unpaved highways were muddy. Our shoes were muddy, we were muddy and sick and hot and thirsty, and then we came to a flood and had to wait and wait. Finally the water went down enough that we could be pulled across the creek by a team and wagon. The man charged five dollars a tow. Dad was outraged, but he paid it, because he had to get his truckload of sick kids home.

It seems insane that Mother would have had a satin and gold brocade hat perched on her head in the middle of a flood in the Panhandle of Texas, but she did. As we were being towed through the rapid current, Virginia, with the genius all four-year-old children have for doing precisely the wrong thing, reached across Mother and jerked open the door. Model A's were not spacious, and Mother and Barbara, who were leaning against the door, almost fell. Mother grabbed Barbara just before she hit the water, but the hat fell from Mother's head, landed upside down in the river, and sailed east. Dad swore, Virginia screamed, Barbara cried, and I watched the hat out of sight. It seemed a jaunty thing going its own way to incredible adventures.

Chapter 3

Cowboys

Henry Nash Smith, in his book *Virgin Land*, gave a list of books and magazines that pertained to the West. He said these writings had greatly influenced the image the world had of cowboys and the image cowboys had of themselves. I'm sure he was right, but I was disappointed with Smith because he did not mention Zane Grey, that great molder of the mythical American cowboy. As I remember my childhood, I know that I saw this myth in the making, and I know that a great deal of the credit for the legend should go to Zane Grey. I have seen photographs of roundups taken sometime in the 1890s. The men in these photographs do not look at all like the cowboys I knew in my childhood. I go back to these pictures from time to time, and I wonder, "Where are the high-heeled boots? Where are the chaps, the tight Levis, and the fancy saddles and bridles?" The men in the photographs look like nesters, yet they were riders for

some of the big spreads, the 101, the JA, and even the XIT.
The cowboys of the 1920s and 1930s were far more glamorous. Their boots were gorgeous, with needle-pointed
heels; large red and green butterflies were appliquéd on
the tops with, I do remember well, four rows of colored
stitching. There had to be four rows, because any row of
stitching above two cost extra, and the four rows were a
mark of status and affluence. At any rate, there was a
difference between the three-row man and the four-row
man. No one I knew was a two-row man.

There were some affluent years on the ranges in the
late 1920s, and cowboys loved to make a good appearance. They spent their money on wonderful horses, silver
mounted saddles and bridles, and tapaderos with thongs
that nearly reached the ground. They all wore Stetson
hats. There are no guns strapped to the sides of the men
in the old pictures, but the cowboys I knew wore six-
guns, and they carried rifles on their saddles. Had anyone
asked them—and of course no one ever did—they would
have said the guns were for varmints, but I have seen
them practice a fast draw and a quick shot, although the
Indians and desperados had long since vanished from
that peaceful valley.

Some of their names come to my mind. Donald
Capansky and his brother Glenn, who played the guitar
for the country dances, and their cousin Charles, who
mounted a piano bench as if it were a horse and played
the piano as if he were gentling a bronc—these men, all
dead now, were first-rate cowboys. Then of course there
are those two quintessential cowboys—those merry men
who, half a century later, will have lived out their legends

Buddy Boy Layton and Jiggs Collins all dressed up to go to a rodeo in Guyman, Oklahoma, 1938. (Photo by LaVerne Hanners, Collection of LaVerne Hanners)

not fifty miles from where they were born. I speak of Jiggs
Collins and Buddy Boy Layton.

Not only were the men of the Cimarron first-rate
cowboys, they were also mighty hunters. They had to be,
especially during the homestead years, and later during
the depression. Families were large, and it was a long
way to the nearest grocery store. A deer hanging on the
north side of a claim shack was a valuable asset.

The meat froze at night and thawed during the day. It
gradually acquired a rind a half-inch thick, and occasionally grew spots of green fungus. When that happened, we washed the haunch down with vinegar. Even
the toughest old buck became tender under repeated
freezing and the aging. It was wonderful meat.

When the Valley was first settled, hunting was as
natural an activity and as regular as fencing, branding, or
any other chore considered necessary for survival. The
passing of the game laws meant only that hunting became fun instead of the hard work it really was. Eluding
the game wardens became the sport of choice for young
men of the Valley.

Wardens swarmed the Cimarron Valley. Although
the warden stationed in Boise City, Oklahoma, had the
entire Cimarron County as his jurisdiction, only the
extreme western end of the Panhandle was rugged
enough for deer. It was the same with the warden stationed in Clayton, New Mexico. This warden could ignore
the flats south of Clayton and concentrate his efforts on
the northern edge of Union County. The Cimarron Valley
was a paradise to poachers and a source of extreme
frustration to the Departments of Game and Fish in both
states.

There were only two roads down into the Valley from Clayton: Highway 18, which came off the top at Reif Hill, and another, smaller road that cut through the cap rock at Travesser. Of course, anyone knowledgeable about country roads could drive right to the cap rock and look down into the Valley at almost any point, but there they were stopped. A warden could hear a high-powered rifle booming in a canyon beneath his feet, could perhaps even detect movement in the brush, and still be helpless. He could, of course, go back to his car, drive through all the gates, come down Reif Hill, drive up the Valley, and eventually arrive at the mouth of the canyon. By this time the hunter would have the deer gutted and hidden securely, to be retrieved after dark.

If the warden made his first approach from the valley floor, the hunter had only to hotfoot it up to the top and sit down in the shade, leaving an enraged warden below him. There were horse trails and footpaths up through the cap rock at several places, but wardens did not like to be separated from their cars, and no game warden was stupid enough to try to pursue a mounted man on foot.

The young men from Kenton, especially, sent the New Mexico Department of Game and Fish into fits of rage. Of these young men from Kenton, Jiggs Collins was the most wanted, most hunted, and most reviled. He was, even at sixteen, a noted poacher and could flit up and down the canyons and over the cap rock like a mountain goat.

He almost got caught once. He and a friend, Walt Glasscock, had left their horses on top to go to the cap rock and peer over the edge. They saw a big buck far below, and Jiggs shot him. He and Walt slithered down the cliff to the deer and cut his throat. At this moment they heard a car door slam and saw beneath them—not far beneath them—the warden's car with four men getting out of it. Jiggs heard the warden yelling, "That's Collins. I know it is. We've got the son of a bitch now."

Jiggs started running up the hill toward the horses out on top. He realized Walt Glasscock was not with him. He looked back down and saw to his horror that Walt had thrown himself behind a rock and was drawing down on the wardens. Jiggs reached Walt in two giant strides and snatched away the gun.

"Oh hell, Jiggs," Walt said. "Let's just shoot them. I ain't going to spend the rest of my life in jail." Jiggs ran back up the hill, carrying two guns under one arm and dragging Walt with the other.

The wardens didn't locate the deer. Jiggs and Walt rode into the ranch about midnight with the deer across Jiggs's saddle. Walt Glasscock always insisted he had no intention of shooting any game wardens. But Jiggs always maintained that, from his point of view, it had looked as if Walt had no intention of missing them, either.

Mother was frying a skillet of venison steaks one day when she looked up and saw John McCandless riding up to the gate. Mother knew he was a lawman of some kind, and panic overtook her. She grabbed the skillet with the tail end of her apron, opened the bedroom door, and slung the skillet—smoking grease, meat, and all—under the bed. She stepped hastily out into the yard to greet Mr. McCandless so he would not come in, at least not until the odor of frying venison had dissipated.

Mr. McCandless got down from his horse and brought out a letter from his inside coat pocket. "Mrs. Goodson, I wish you would read this letter and tell me what it means. It seems to say that I've lost my job."

Mother read the letter and handed it back. "Yes, Mr. McCandless, that is what it says. It's right there. They will no longer need your services after the first of the month. I'm awfully sorry."

John McCandless visibly slumped. I, of course, was watching, and it was that reaction that impressed the incident on my memory. He tipped his hat to Mother and said, "I'm much obliged, Ma'am. I just wanted to be sure." He got back on his horse and rode away.

I called Jiggs and asked him about John McCandless. Jiggs was able to tell me that he was a range detective, hired by a cattlemen's association. Jiggs also told me he was known by the nickname of Scandalous John.

Scandalous John rode a big bay horse and had a magnificent handlebar mustache. The horse and the mustache were already obsolete, and so was Scandalous John's occupation. The times no longer required that a man ride the range looking for rustlers.

I was impressed that he had come to ask my mother about the letter, but after all she was the schoolteacher. Teachers were held in such respect in those days that John McCandless made a long ride horseback just in the faint hope that Mother would be able to deny what he already knew was devastating news. I don't believe we ever saw him again.

It must have been shortly after World War I that the cowboy became enamored of his own myth and began to try to live up to it. I was born in 1921, and we moved to New Mexico from Colorado in 1925. The myth of the spur-jingling cowboy was full-blown then, and the image did not change, at least in that remote corner of New Mexico, until 1941.

No one ever thinks of the cowboy as a reader, but he was. What else was he going to do those long winter nights in the bunkhouse? My younger brother and I taught ourselves to read when I was five and he was four. He used to sneak the cowboys' magazines out of the bunkhouse, and somehow we stumbled through them. I was delighted with the list of magazines in *Virgin Land*, for I remembered them, especially the *Wild West Weekly*. I even remember some of the stories. Billy West and his pard, Monk, were special heroes to the cowboys and to us. I feel sure that these stories and the books of Zane Grey shaped the images the cowboys had of themselves, and I cannot believe that this shaping did them any harm.

At one time I intended to write a volume of poems about cowboys who had achieved at least local fame. When Bill Sutton died at the age of eighty-five, I received a call in the middle of the night, asking if I had not written a poem about him, and if I would send it so that it might be read at his funeral. I knew Bill only after he was quite old—eighty-two, I believe—and was working on the ranch that joined us on the east. My young son and I hunted deer with him, and he told me how he used to make extra money topping out broncs for the other cowboys. He told me how he had become a Christian, gave me a little tract, then brought down a running deer at a quarter of a mile, quite illegally of course. This is the poem I wrote about him.

Bill Sutton

Bill Sutton was a bronc-riding cowboy,
Skilled and willed in riding a horse.
He was thrown once in eighty-two years
By a renegade bronc with the bit in his teeth.

Fractured a leg and with a rib through a lung,
Was carried forty miles in a wagon.
Jesus and Bill held a long parley
Made their bargain and Bill was healed.

He walked thereafter in the steps of his Master,
And every day was Sunday for Bill.

Bill worked and ate and rode with the others
Worked and played and sang and prayed.
Bill walked tall and proud on the earth,
And nobody never said "Nigger" to Bill.

I really knew two different sets of cowboys, the older ones, some of whom are in the old photographs, and the younger ones, who were involved in their own legend. When Bill Sutton rode a bronc he did it because he was paid a dollar to do it, and the others felt no shame at all in having Bill top out a bad horse on a frosty morning. The boys and men who were my contemporaries would have died before they asked someone else to ride a horse for them. They rode broncs because tradition said they must, and they rode in competition with one another. In that day, every little community had its rodeo, and each had its champion rider. Johnny Like was the hero of all the riders,

Neighborhood rodeo at True Benton's ranch up on top of the south mesas between the Valley and Clayton, New Mexico. Jiggs Collins on top of the chute, getting ready to ride a bull, ca. 1938. (Photo by LaVerne Hanners. Collection of LaVerne Hanners)

because he rode with a tight rein and a short stirrup and he still outrode them all.

Johnny Like and J. B. King held a match calf roping one time. They each roped and tied ten calves. The men were pretty evenly matched, but J. B. King had a little bit better luck. His time for the ten calves was three or four seconds better than Johnny Like's time.

Loser or no, no one who watched that roping could have doubted that Johnny Like's horse was the best. He was a hard-twisted little blue horse named, naturally, Old Blue, and he could have switched ends in a bushel basket. He could pivot on one hind foot. J. B. coveted Johnny's horse.

"Say, Johnny, what'll you take for the horse?"

"Oh, J. B., I can't sell you my horse. I need him."

"Name your price. Just name it, and I'll get you the money."

"No, now dad gum it, I told you I couldn't sell you my horse. I have to have him."

"Well, how come? Why won't you sell me that horse?"

Johnny looked J. B. straight in the eye and said, "J. B., I got a herd of prairie dogs back at the ranch, and they're just about ready to wean, and this old blue horse here is the only one I've got that can cut those prairie dogs away from their holes."

J. B. threw up his hands in disgust. "Just go ahead and keep your damned old horse then. You need him a lot worse than I do."

Cowboys loved competition. They strove to outrun, outrope, and outride each other. Shirley Labrier was the acknowledged champion foot racer in the Valley. He outran everyone who challenged him, and he ran from a standing start.

Finally they imported a track star from Las Cruces. I don't know who organized the race or what they hoped to prove by it, but the race was set, the hundred yards was carefully measured, and I expect a few bets were placed.

The young college man was astonished that his opponent would race from a standing position. He said, "Well, he may outrun me, but if he does he'll have to catch me, 'cause there isn't a man alive who can stand up and beat me off the blocks."

The starter fired the gun and the track star came up out of his runner's crouch to see Shirley's back drawing away. The young man managed to catch and pass Shirley right at the wire. He went on back to Las Cruces, but before he left he was heard several times wondering just how fast that tall, skinny cowboy would have been if he had ever had any training.

Walter Hanners was another foot racer. He could outrun very nearly everyone with the notable exception of Shirley Labrier. Once at a community picnic there was a matched race set up between two young men who were long on ambition but short on experience. They asked Walter to start the race, and gave him the starting gun. Then someone said, "Who will we get to judge the finish?"

Walter said, "I will. I'll start them and run down there and judge the finish."

Everyone laughed, a judge was picked, and Walter fired the starting gun. The judge watched in amazement as three men pounded toward him. Walter reached the finish line, whirled around, and pointed at the first man coming up. "You win," he said.

The differing competitions, at least for that part of the cowboy West, took the place of the heroics of the gun battle and the Indian fight, but I do not mean to imply that these men were in any way fakes. They were working cowboys, and danger was a very real part of their lives. Some of this danger, no doubt, could have been avoided.

Tooter Davis (I have no idea of his Christian name) distinguished himself by bulldogging a buck deer, hog-tying it, and bringing it home across his saddle. He tied the deer to the windmill, and people came from far and wide to see the deer and Tooter, who was really quite a sight. As he explained it, "That old buck just jumped up right by my horse, so I fell off on him and grabbed him by the horns. He damn near kicked me to ribbons." Tooter's big stud, Red Pick, later killed Tooter by bolting under a low-hanging branch of a cottonwood tree. Nobody ever had trusted that horse, it seemed, although he got very fine colts.

My oldest brother, John, nearly lost his life on a cattle drive when he was twelve. He was a corner man on a rope corral. A running horse hit the rope and, in some sort of freakish way, jerked it out of Johnny's hand. The rope whipped around his neck. The other cowboys swore that Johnny spun like a top when the rope was then jerked off his neck. It should have torn his head off, but although he still has some scars, it only rope-burned him from his lower lip to his collarbone.

Cattlemen are the funniest people in the world. One might not think so to see them in a bunch, talking slowly, using very few gestures, and smiling not at all. They seem very serious, but really they are only waiting for a turn. Western people cherish the quip, the well-turned phrase, or a different and unusual way of saying things. One foreman had composed a little jingle he used for rousting the cowboys out of the bunkhouse. He would stick his head in the door and yell, "Okay, you cowboys grab your chaps and taps and latigo straps and get on out of here! It's nearly daylight!" Chaps, of course, were the leather leggings that went on over the Levis, "taps" was short for tapaderos, the leather shields that covered the stirrups, and a latigo was the strap one used to tighten a cinch. This foreman derived an almost mystical pleasure from his little incantation, but the cowboys hated it, probably because the foreman thought of it first.

Miller Easley had a cowboy holler. If it was a particularly cold day, Miller hollered at people when they came into his store: "Hey, how would you like to be up on that point with nothing on but a wet nightgown and a pair of spurs?" This chilling question produced two results. Men scrooched down and sheltered their laps with their hands. Women wrapped their arms across their breasts.

Once Buddy Boy Layton's wife, Deloryse, and I had sewn a dozen choir robes for the church choir. It had been a stupefying chore, and we were anxious for approval. We showed our handiwork to Buddy Boy. He muttered something noncommittal, and I got mad.

"The trouble with you, Buddy Layton, is that you just aren't very easily impressed."

Buddy Boy stared thoughtfully into the distance, then said, "I went in on Normandy Beach on D-Day. That impressed me."

These throwaway lines of Bud's have stayed with me for over forty years. Whenever I see anyone try to overwhelm others with his own importance, I think, "Well, that sure wouldn't impress Bud Layton." And when I find myself trying a grandstand act, I can get back my per-spective by thinking, "What are you trying to do, impress Bud Layton?"

The humor of the cowboy is dry, subtle, and generally makes a point no one but a cowboy would have thought of. I am thinking in particular of Ben Walker, an old cowman who rode for many, many years for George Wiggins. Ben was getting a little too old for the hard work on the ranch, so the bright idea occurred to George to get Ben a small herd of sheep to take care of. Ben was a real cowboy, and he was separated from his horse only when he ate or slept. His method of herding sheep was some-what different from that practiced by most people who know the ways of sheep. To Ben a herd was a compact unit, so he took his sheep out, bunched them in a corner of the pasture fence, and loped his horse in a tight half-circle around the sheep. Ben was changing horses three times a day.

Buddy Boy was cowboying for George while all this was going on, and he took the job of keeping the herd together while Ben went in for food or a fresh horse. Buddy Boy said that occasionally an old ewe would break out of the circle and try to get to grass, but Ben was quicker. He herded her smartly back to the bunch.

Several weeks passed, and one morning Ben came in to see George. "George, do you still want me to go on herding sheep for you?"

George looked up, startled. "Why sure, Ben, of course I do."

Ben sighed. "Well, George, I guess you better get me some more sheep, then. I just about got these all herded up."

George knew with certainty that if he didn't take quick action his days as a woolgrower were numbered. He said, "Well, Ben, maybe you better go on out with the other boys, and I'll see if I can get Lee Henley to lend us a hand." Lee came up and took over the few sheep that were left. He took them to good grass and water and soon had a thriving herd. And Ben, having convinced George that he was no sheepherder, continued as a cowboy.

Some of the funniest incidents occurred when a cowboy was confronted by a tenderfoot. The cowboy felt called upon to treat that person with courtesy, but if the tenderfoot asked some particularly asinine question this was pretty hard to do. A young girl fresh from the East was visiting on my father's ranch once. She turned to Fred Claflin, the oldest and dourest cowboy on the ranch. "Tell me, Mr. Claflin, how many cattle does it take to have a stampede?"

Fred was considerably taken aback, but after a slight struggle came up with an answer. "Well, Miss, I guess you could have a stampede with just one." Then he thought a minute longer, grinned, and said, "But it wouldn't get scattered out very much."

Incidents that involved a funny saying, like Ben Walker's herded-up sheep or Fred Claflin's one-cow stampede, became legends. Other legends involved people who did or said funny things inadvertently. One such character was Ant Stomping Jake. Ant Stomping Jake was a full-grown man, but his mind had remained in blissful childhood. He had two great pleasures in life. He stomped ants and he chopped wood. The cowboys loved to point out ants to Jake, and sometimes even pointed out ants that didn't exist. It didn't matter to Jake. If Jake thought there were ants, real or imaginary, he went into his high-stepping erratic dance.

Jake more than earned his keep by chopping wood. If he was given an ax and shown the woodpile, he would happily chop wood and stack it up ready for the stove. Once the family left for town, all the cowboys had ranch chores to do, and Jake was left alone. It is likely he stomped ants for a while and then, as there was no one to applaud, grew bored with that. He got his ax and went to the woodpile, but there were no logs left unchopped. His eyes lit upon the windmill. When the family came home, Jake was chopping up the last leg of the windmill, and the rest of it was neatly stacked up for firewood.

Jake's family replaced the old wooden windmill with a metal one, and saw to it thereafter that Jake had plenty of logs to work with.

Walter Hanners told the story of the cowboy who was trying to remember his manners when he had eaten a company dinner. The cowboy reached into his pocket for his bandanna to use for a napkin, and saw too late that he had pulled out his spare pair of socks and was patting his mouth with them. Already demoralized by that mistake, the cowboy turned to his hostess and said, "Well, Ma'am, that sure was a good dinner, what there was of it." He realized that didn't sound right and tried to correct himself. "No, I mean there was plenty, such as it was."

Walter also told about visiting another cowboy at a line cabin. The young man had brought a bucket of water from the creek. He poured some in the coffeepot and the rest into the dishpan and heated it on the wood stove. He washed his and Walter's dishes; he washed out his dish towel; he washed a couple of pair of socks. Then he put the pan on the floor, got out his mop, and scrubbed the cabin floor.

Walter watched all this and then told him, "You know, Jim, you don't use water up, you wear it out."

One of my favorite western stories concerns the old blacksmith and the fellow who was always meddling around the blacksmith shop. He nearly drove the black-smith crazy getting in his way, picking things up, and asking silly questions. One day the blacksmith heated a horseshoe just under red hot and put it out where the pest would be sure to see it. Sure enough, the man came along, picked up the horseshoe, and of course quickly dropped it on the ground.

The old blacksmith, very seriously and without cracking a grin, said, "What's the matter, burn yourself?"

"No, no," the other replied. "It just doesn't take me very long to look at a horseshoe."

It seems the more serious a situation is the more jokes are made about it. Some of the best stories of the West were circulated during the Great Drought and Depression of the thirties. The cowman joked about everything, even his desperate struggle to obtain money against a blown-out ranch and a herd of starving cattle. I suppose every poor harassed banker in the West had this story told about him. An old cattleman went in to the banker to try to obtain a little more money for feed. He explained his situation, that it hadn't rained for two years, his cattle weren't worth anything, and he couldn't sell them anyway for there were no buyers. His kids were all hungry, his wife was sick, and he just had to have a little more money.

The banker looked at him and said, "Well, Slim, I

really shouldn't give you any more money, because you have already borrowed more than your ranch and cattle are worth, but I'll tell you what. I have one glass eye, and it's a real good one. No one has ever been able to say which of my eyes is glass. I'll make you the loan if you can tell me which it is."

The cowman said without hesitation, "Your right eye is glass."

The banker was astonished. "That is right. But how in the world did you know?"

The cowman said, "Well, when I was telling you my sad story, there was once when I thought I could detect a little gleam of sympathy in that right eye."

Then of course there is the story of the droughted-out rancher who was caught in a light sprinkle of rain. He fainted and they had to pour two buckets of sand on him to bring him around.

Cattlemen have ways of giving directions that are funny, completely clear, and unforgettable. I was taught how to make coffee by a cowboy who lived in the Cimarron Valley and who drank his coffee black and strong. His name was Carroll Simpson, and his recipe for coffee was simple. I was appointed to make the coffee for the get-together at the Goodson School. As I started to measure out the coffee, Carroll came over. "Now," he said, "I'll tell you how to make good coffee. First measure out just exactly the amount of coffee you think you need." I measured out what I thought was enough and looked to Carroll for further instructions. "Now, put in just exactly that much more coffee."

When I got the coffee poured in the water, Carroll concluded his lesson by saying, "It just doesn't take near as much water to make coffee as everyone thinks it does.''

Some of the best western stories were outrageous but also quite true. Some were simply outrageous. And many were told at the expense of people who the storytellers thought took themselves, perhaps, too seriously.

Albert Mitchell was a rancher who was well-known not only in New Mexico but wherever cattle were raised. He was always a very busy man, especially during World War II, when he served in an advisory capacity in Washington. He was so busy in national affairs that he hardly had time for his own business of ranching. Albert Mitchell's many and varied activities, his business and his busy-ness, were the basis for a story that was told widely and with great glee by his rancher neighbors. It seems that it was spring roundup time on the Mitchell Ranch and Albert had just flown in from Washington to help with the work. He slept a few hours and then rushed out to get the roundup started. He rounded up the north pasture. He rounded up the south pasture. Then, as he was halfway through rounding up the east pasture, he saw a calf with screwworms that had to be cut out from the herd. He reached down to get his rope from his saddle and discovered that he had forgotten his horse.

Whether the love of outrageous practical jokes was a part of the cowboy myth I do not know, but practical jokes were a part of the tradition of both generations of cowboys. This tradition was no doubt helped along by tales of jokes and ridiculous pranks that were printed in magazines, but the cowboys I knew had great originality in such matters and a fine disregard for their own safety. Juan Nugent beat his two young nephews, Buddy Boy and

Doug Layton, blue with his cinch after he finally caught them. He had been forced to cut off his brand new boots after they had poured a little molasses in each boot.

No punitive action was taken against Jiggs Collins, because no one knew that a sudden rash of bobcats that appeared in a small and peaceful town was not a natural phenomenon. The bobcats decimated the stray dog and cat population of the town before Jiggs gallantly organized a posse to hunt them down. Oddly enough, it did not occur to anyone that Jiggs, who was trapping for the government, might have had anything to do with the bobcats' appearance in the first place. This happened not too long ago, and Jiggs certainly should have known better.

Jiggs was much younger when he and Lumpy were riding for the Harris Ranch. The foreman, Ed Towers, was a good old man, as Jiggs told it, but he did have the annoying habit of sicking his big English bulldog on the hands as they went about their work. Old Tige had lifted large mouthfuls out of every cowboy on the place. Jiggs and Lumpy rode into town one night and got drunk. They rode back home and were unsaddling when Tige grabbed Lumpy right above the boot top. Jiggs kicked Tige loose and took down his rope. He roped Tige and hog-tied him, and he and Lumpy took the wire pliers and pulled every tooth in the dog's head. Ed was mad, but he didn't fire them. He made it one of their daily chores to grind Tige's food up in the sausage grinder.

At the beginning of the twentieth century, Doctor Lane came to the little town of Kenton, Oklahoma, and set up practice. She must have been one of the first women doctors, and why she came to the isolated Valley no one ever knew, but she did come and she delivered babies all up and down the Valley. Kenton, at the very western end of the Panhandle of Oklahoma, was at that time still very much a frontier town, and the doctor had considerable work bandaging up gunshot wounds and other mayhem that the citizens had visited on one another.

One day, when Doctor Lane was still new to the community, Cappy (absolutely not his correct name), who had been chosen for his role by God knows what primitive ritual, detached himself from a group of men and strolled over to Doctor Lane's office. The conversation went something like this.

"Yes, Mr. Cappy, what can I do for you?"

Cappy dropped his pants and said, "Doctor Lane, I just wish you'd take a look at my pecker."

Doctor Lane carefully examined the object in question and said, "Why, Mr. Cappy, I don't find a thing wrong."

"Oh, I know," Cappy sighed, "but ain't it a dandy?"

Doctor Lane broke her office chair over Cappy's head, and then helped him up on the table and sewed up a large gash on his head. Twenty years later, when I knew Cappy, the scar was still dreadful, but I think the rumor that she sewed him up with sash cord is only local folklore.

At first it seemed the episode of Cappy and Doctor Lane was a link between the younger cowboys and the older ones and illustrated the love they all had for the practical joke, but as I think of it, I realize that no cowboy true to the tradition of Nevada, or of Arizona Ames, or of Billy West, would ever have been a part of this joke. Some more elemental force was at work—the myth of the dominant male and the subservient woman. It also has, in its blatant sexuality, a stark assertion of power, thinly disguised to the men themselves as a practical joke. There are, too, certain aspects of the rite of initiation. If so, Doctor Lane, in her initial reaction of outraged womanhood and her reassertion of her "male" role as doctor, passed the test. After the others saw Cappy stagger out of Doctor Lane's office with his head banged up, she was never challenged again.

The later generation of cowboys all laughed when anyone mentioned Cappy's encounter with justice, but the most truly cherished story of all time concerned O'Dell and his horse. Every horseman knows you can ride a horse up a hill that you cannot ride him down, but no one has ever investigated this basic premise more thoroughly than did O'Dell Harris. O'Dell got drunk one night in Amarillo, Texas, and rode his horse up four flights of stairs to his bedroom in the Herring Hotel. O'Dell tied the horse to the foot of the bed and went to sleep.

The next morning the police hauled O'Dell off to jail, and then began the struggle to get the horse out of the hotel. The horse, evidently in the grips of a massive seizure of acrophobia, absolutely refused to be ridden, led, or carried back down the stairs. A crowd gathered and the Society for the Prevention of Cruelty to Animals arrived on the scene. Someone suggested shooting the horse and taking him out piecemeal, but this suggestion was sternly vetoed by both the SPCA and O'Dell, who had posted a sizable bail and arrived back at the hotel. O'Dell swore that he would kill anyone who harmed his best roping horse, and I actually believe that the idea was never given serious consideration because, after all, a good roping horse was an extremely valuable animal and not lightly destroyed. They finally took out a window and part of a wall and, with the aid of a crane and a sling, lowered the horse to the ground. O'Dell's hotel bill was astronomical.

The cowboys, of course, were wildly envious of O'Dell's well-publicized feat and took some of the glory themselves, but to my knowledge no one tried to duplicate it. Copying someone's else's joke was not in the tradition. Originality was prized almost as highly as personal bravery; copying would have been scorned as much as cowardice.

The image of personal bravery and fortitude in danger surely stood the young men I knew in good stead during World War II. All of them enlisted and, amazingly, all of them returned. Some won great honors; Juan Nugent won every medal but the Congressional, and all returned amply beribboned. My younger brother, Felix, who is a professor of psychology at DePauw, might not agree with me, but I cannot help believing that the cowboy legend of bravery, endurance, and resourcefulness must have had some shaping influence upon him that enabled him to survive the whole war in a Japanese prison camp.

I do not know if there has ever been a study done of the role of the working cowboy in World War II, but I should imagine that such a study would reveal a great influence upon him of the myth of the heroic cowboy. It occurs to me that World War II was for these men the last great Indian battle, and in a way it may have been the last heroic battle of all time. The atomic bomb exploded that myth along with Hiroshima.

Virgin Land traces the myths of the frontier as they

were developed in the popular writings of the nineteenth century. The works of James Fenimore Cooper, says Henry Nash Smith, were the prototypes of a genre of western fiction that idealized the simple heroic son of the forest and established myths that are still discernible in television programs and western paperbacks. However much these Cooper legends and traditions did shape the West of the cattleman—and they were a major influence—the pulp magazines and the novels of Owen Wister and Zane Grey also had a great influence on the lives of the cowboys.

So for a while it was really true. Cowboys did sit around the bunkhouses, play harmonicas and guitars, and sing the long, mournful cowboy ballads in which women were incredibly pure, men handsome and brave, and horses swift and gallant. The cowboys did come into town every Saturday night and get drunk and go to dances and get into fistfights and go to jail. Jiggs Collins had a cowboy yell that could peel the paint off a barn, and when it reverberated down the streets and alleys of the little cowtown of Clayton, New Mexico, Pop Hanners, the night marshal, would put his head in his hands and moan, "Oh, God, not again," and then go out and gather him in. The cowboy hero did exist in the time between the two world wars. He may have invented himself out of materials furnished by Zane Grey, Owen Wister, and others. But he thought he was real. He was real, whatever his sources.

Chapter 4

The Children

The children of the Valley, in that time between the two world wars, were especially blessed. There weren't many of us, but when I compare the Valley then to the deserted Valley of today it seems that in those days it teemed with life. On our end of the Valley there were five Goodsons, four Wigginses, one Rutledge, four Behimers, and various other children from time to time as families moved in, then moved away and were replaced by others.

There were three schools in the lower end of the Valley—the New Mexico School, the Wagner School, and the Valley School. These schools were all in different districts and were six to ten miles apart. We lived on the old Roberts Ranch when we first came to the Valley. We joined the Wiggins Ranch on the east. The two ranches were both in the New Mexico School district, and the Goodson and Wiggins children were the permanent population of the school. Wagner and New Mexico schools were taught by Kathryn Quimby and my mother. They switched schools from time to time, perhaps because of enrollment. If Wagner School ran short of children, Mother taught there and took a child or two with her.

There had to be an enrollment of eight children for a school to stay open. If George Wiggins, Shorty Quimby, or Felix Goodson was hiring men to work with the alfalfa on the river or cattle on the ranges, their first question had to do with the man's family and how many children the family would contribute toward keeping the school open.

Usually there were enough children to open the school, but once, before my youngest sister, Barbara, and the younger Wiggins girl, Shirley, were old enough to go to school, we fell short. The first day of school Mother looked out over her classroom and saw only her four oldest children and three Wigginses. She glanced up toward the fence where the Wiggins's horse was tied. She picked up her attendance register and wrote firmly, "Danny Wiggins." The New Mexico School may be the only school in the United States that graduated a horse from the eighth grade.

Of course after Mother had perpetrated this mild fraud against the state of New Mexico there was no way she could get out of it, so year after year went by with Danny Wiggins, ever faithful in attendance, maintaining a C average. He graduated the year before the schools were consolidated.

I'm sure George and Margaret Wiggins and Shorty and Kathryn Quimby were in cahoots with Mother and Dad over this deception, as it would have been a disaster if any of the schools had closed. There were no school buses in those days, and no provisions made for the

isolated child. Registering a horse must have made good
sense to the patrons of the school. Of course no one
spoke of the arrangement, and I knew only after Mother
told me about it many years later, when she was in her
eighties.

When my brothers and I first started, the school term
was only seven months long. We were released to glorious freedom during the first week in April, with five
months ahead of us, the whole Valley to play with, and
horses.

We rode quite astonishing distances, visiting each
other's homes and drifting by one house or the other at
noon, where we hoped to be asked to eat. We were always
invited in. About our only rule was that we had to be home
by sundown, and we always were, at whatever cost.

Once Felix had ridden Peewee over to the Wiggins
Ranch. It was getting late and Felix started home. There
had been a cloud hanging back up the Valley for some
time. Dad called George, and George went to find Felix
and tell him he was to stay the night, but Felix was
nowhere to be found. "Oh, he's gone home," Jimmy said.

George drove to the river crossing and got there just
in time to see Felix jump Peewee out into a full-bank flood
that was raging down the Cimarron. Felix was clinging
like a burr to Peewee's mane. Logs careered by them in
front and in back. Once both their heads went under
while George watched in horror. Felix and Peewee made
it to the opposite bank. Felix looked back, waved merrily
at George, and started for home at a run. The sun was
almost down.

I can't imagine how it was that we had such freedom.
I suppose our parents thought there was nothing in the

Valley that could hurt us, and if we were on our horses and gone at least we weren't under foot. Our parents didn't realize, of course, that we were all doing very dangerous things. We raced our horses across the Valley floor, through prairie-dog towns, and across ditches. We swam in the river and we body surfed the Bontz Arroyo when it flooded. We climbed the cap rock on the Black Mesa.

One little deathtrap Dad himself provided for us. He built a new concrete water storage tank, then decided it was too dangerous, so he put a roof over it. The men left a little trapdoor down into the tank. When Mother was busy and Dad was gone, my brothers and I checked the whereabouts of the hands. If all was clear we eased the trapdoor up a bit and slid like eels into the dark water, clothes and all. If the tank was full we had only four inches' clearance between the water and the roof. This was fine for swimming on our backs, and we all became adept at that. Swimming face down required the ability to hold one's breath a goodish long time. We had to flip over on our backs to breathe. After we swam, we slipped over to the garden hose and sprayed each other down so we could legitimately tell Mother we had had a water fight — a permitted activity.

We climbed trees. The Roberts place was graced with enormous silver leaf maples, and one huge cottonwood in the corner of the garden. Those trees looked like heaven to children who had lived only on the treeless plains of Colorado. We went up them like a bunch of monkeys. The top limbs of those wonderful trees became part of our natural habitat. Mother said she looked out the kitchen window and saw Felix astride a slender branch some thirty feet from the ground. He didn't seem to be in any distress, so Mother wisely let him be. He was only four years old, and if she had yelled at him and startled him he could have fallen.

She and Marion Collins were not so wise when they yelled at their two little boys, Felix, five, and Mike, four, for engaging in a bizarre ritual. I heard about the episode when it happened, but not until a year ago when Felix told me about it did I understand the details. Felix tied a string around the head of Mike's penis and then tied the other end of the string around the head of his own. They stood there, grinning happily at this childish bonding. When Marion and Mother spotted them, unfortunately they yelled.

When Mother and Marion shouted, Mike started to run. Felix saw what was going to happen, so he grabbed the string in the middle and braced. Mike hit the end of the string. It tightened and sank deep into the flesh. The women carried Mike into the house, where he screamed until they finally got the string cut.

Felix was a strange little boy, redheaded and freckle faced. He was something of a loner, needing space and time to work out his schemes. One of his schemes involved dynamite caps.

I had taken the box of caps from the ledge under the roof of the garage. Dad had put them there in what he imagined was absolute security. To get them I climbed up on a workbench on the opposite side of the building; then I hauled myself up into the open rafters that supported the low roof. I crawled across the rafters, tucked the small, round box under my chin, and made my way back. Felix and I hid the caps in one of our many hideouts.

Felix also later told me what happened to the dynamite caps. He slipped out of the house early one morning, retrieved the caps, and headed for the Black Mesa. He walked two miles to the foot of that towering mesa, then started his long climb upwards. He went through the cap rock on the Wiggins trail, a horse-wide path that George Wiggins had built to give access to the pasturelands on top of the mesa. Felix reached the top and walked along the cap rock until he found the perfect place. He stood there on the edge of the cap rock, scared but determined. Then he threw the dynamite caps as far as he could. The small box sailed up, then down again, to disappear under the edge of the cap rock. Felix waited, and waited. Absolutely nothing happened.

Felix said, "It was one of the great disappointments of my life. I was sure there would be an explosion that would rock the world, but there was nothing. Just nothing. I went back down the Mesa and on home."

I knew how he felt. Some of our great plans were not successful because of our ignorance of the laws of physics, but we really did try.

There was a little rock knoll just behind the schoolhouse we attended. The schoolhouse was on the downhill slope of the knoll. Right on top of the little hill there was a rock at least four feet high and about four feet across on a rock pedestal about a foot thick. The rock on top was quite round. We started to work on that rock. First we sawed through the pedestal. It was no easy chore, for we were sawing with barb wire and the wire kept wearing out. This meant that we had to go farther and farther afield to get more wire. We knew that it would not be a good idea to take too much from one place. We were taking the bottom wire from fences.

We sawed. The going was slow, but with the tenacity of children or the feebleminded we kept it up. Two months went by. Christmas came and went. At last the wire went completely through the pedestal. The rock was loose. The great day had arrived. We all got behind the rock and pushed. Slowly and ponderously the great stone toppled from its pedestal. It crashed off a little ledge, rolled to the bottom of the hill, turned over twice, and stopped, still a hundred feet from the schoolhouse.

I don't believe we really thought that huge boulder would smash through the schoolhouse. In my mind's eye I saw the stone hurtling down the slope and on out into the flat, going like a meteor. I thought it would be so grand, and it just wasn't.

I am still not sure what high-life is. It is, I know, a liquid that is used in some manner to kill prairie dogs. It evaporates rapidly. In the fur of an animal or on a human head this evaporation gives a sensation of extreme cold. We all tried it out in minute amounts. It was so cold we felt we were burning, but it was bearable when one knew what was coming. Of course, the poor pigs and the cat had no forewarning. The things those animals did when even a small amount was poured on them astonished even us. There is no excusing the cruelty of children, but the high-life left no marks at all, so I don't think we realized how bad we were being. I think that the idea of filling water pistols with high-life belongs to Felix. In fact, as I look back, most of our better efforts were the products of the fertile mind of my little redheaded brother. I am sure that when he was captured by the Japanese at the age of seventeen, no one in the Valley really worried about Felix. They seemed to think that it served the Japanese right. They were sure Felix would get home all right, which he did, but that those Japanese had better watch out.

So it was that we all armed ourselves with pistols filled with high-life. The first one to catch it was the cat. Felix squirted a pistol full of high-life down her back, and the cat leaped ten feet into the air and tore through the kitchen door right on through the washing- machine motor and between my mother's legs, circled the walls of the kitchen like one of those midget racers going around a steep bowl racetrack, leaped from the top of the cabinet to the stove, and from there ran back out the kitchen door and up a tree, while my mother watched in popeyed amazement.

My dad's special concern was his pigs. He had several shoats in the fattening pen, which had a board fence around it. That fence meant absolutely nothing to those pigs when we got them with the high-life. They went through it and over it as though it were paper. The hired hand kept adding boards to the fence, but still at intervals the pigs would break out and go tearing across the alfalfa fields.

Dad told about his pigs far and wide across the countryside. He used to say with wonder in his voice, "Why, do you know I've got pigs that can stand flat-footed and jump a six-foot fence." He used to stand for hours beside the pen hoping to catch them in the act, but he never did. While Dad watched them they would all huddle peacefully in the corner. A careful observer might even have said that they were cowering in the corner.

Finally Fred Claflin must have sensed there was

something going on that could be prevented, for he watched and finally caught Felix sneaking up on the pigs. He waited until Felix had high-lifed the hogs, then pounced. He took Felix out behind the barn and administered the thrashing that we all should have shared. Then he sent word to the rest of us that we had better blinkety-blank well not do that again and if we would promise not to he would not tell our folks. I have often wondered how Fred came to be so generous, but I think he must have thought that if he did tell on us there was a possibility he might lose his group of poker players.

Fred was an inveterate poker player, but in the long winters when he was the only hand on the place there wasn't anyone to play with. So he gathered us kids. John, Felix, and I learned to play poker before we learned to read. We learned it well, too. Fred would stand for no shilly-shallying. We played heads-up poker every bit as earnestly as if we were playing for dollars instead of matches. It seems strange, looking back, to think of my five-year-old brother sitting there, steely eyed and frozen faced, bluffing us out of our matches with a busted flush.

There never was a greater time for children. The First World War was safely over. The atomic bomb was not yet even a dim cloud on the horizon. The depression had not yet arrived, and when it did we were not aware of it. Parents in the Valley did not give children a lot of cash anyway, and we always had plenty to eat. The occasional nickel to buy a double ice-cream cone at the parlor in Kenton was riches.

Best of all, we were raised by cowboys. This was a little like being raised by wolves, but we learned so many things. Cowboys were not hampered by theories of education, nor did they mind swearing. The three old cow-boys on the place were Fred Claflin, Old Man Coe, and Bartolo Viejo. Fred was the foreman and principal of our rough-and-ready school of survival on the Cimarron. He taught us to ride. We could all stay on horses, but Fred taught the finer points, like getting on. "First," he said, "take the reins in your left hand. Now put that left hand on the horse's mane. Grab the saddle horn with your right hand, stick your left foot in the stirrup, and swing up. That way, if the horse bolts before you're all the way up, he will pull you into the saddle."

It's true. I see cowboys in western movies grab the saddle horn with their left hand and the cantle with their right. Then they stick a foot between their hands and get on board the horse in this inelegant manner. Their rear ends are hanging out, and if the horse moved a muscle those rear ends would be grass. Of course, movie horses never bolt—or if they do we never see it.

It was well that we had Fred to help us with our horses. He was able to take some of the curse off Dad's choice of mounts for his children.

Dad was born in a large city in the South and did not come west until he was a man grown. Sometimes his ideas of what was right and proper for a child to have were colored by his childhood in the city and bore no real relationship to the actual needs, or even wishes, of the five children he was raising out in the West.

For one thing, my father had the idiotic idea that Shetland ponies were far better for children to learn to ride than our regular-sized cow ponies. He must have reasoned that if we fell it wasn't very far to the ground. In this, he was absolutely right. However, as I look back I can see that his knowledge of the Shetland pony stopped right there. His ignorance of the workings of their peculiar little minds was lamentable.

The morning my brother John was six years old, Dad led him outside. There, tied to the fence by the reins of a brand new bridle and sporting a brand new Jim Dean saddle (small size), was Peewee. Peewee was a pinto: sorrel and white. He stood about waist-high to a short man. He had beautiful, dreamy brown eyes that only occasionally flickered with an evil gleam. He was wonderful, a perfect little miniature of a horse. My dad was completely taken in.

"There he is, son. His name is Peewee, and he's just the same age you are." Dad untied the reins from the fence and handed them to John with a flourish. "Now you won't have to walk to school any more."

While it was true that in years John and Peewee were twins, John was certainly not equal to the sophistication that Peewee had picked up in six years. My brother was just a child, a tender, innocent little boy. Peewee was already a hardened sinner, a concentrated little bundle of frustration and maladjustment, wise far beyond his years.

My younger brother, Felix, and I went out to the corral with John the next morning to wave good-bye to him as he went to school and also to watch him saddle Peewee. John had started early, which was a good thing. He threw the saddle on Peewee and tightened the cinch. The saddle was good and tight. John had shaken it by the saddle horn before he tried to get on. He put a foot in the stirrup and started to swing aboard. The saddle turned and John fell under the pony. Peewee lashed out with a back foot and missed, due to the incredibly fast reflexes of a six-year-old boy. John pushed the saddle up on Peewee's back again. There were now about three inches of space between the cinch and Peewee's belly. John started to tighten the cinch again. All three of us became aware at the same time that Peewee was methodically pumping himself full of air. We watched in awe while Peewee blew himself up like a balloon. John's lips thinned to the grim line that was to become habitual with him.

"LaVerne, you hold the reins. Felix, when I tell you, you kick him in the belly." John grabbed the cinch strap with both hands. "Now!" he cried. Felix delivered a hearty kick in the middle of Peewee's belly. Peewee exhaled with a gust that nearly blew me over, and John tightened the cinch strap three whole spaces.

Peewee's head dropped. He seemed defeated. John again put a foot in the stirrup and was swinging up when Felix screamed, "Look out!" Peewee's head whipped around like a striking snake. His teeth were bared. John missed having a cup-sized bite taken out of his ankle by repeatedly kicking Peewee in the jaw.

Felix and I stood entranced at the language that poured out of John's mouth. Felix was four years old and I was five, and it was only rarely that we heard such inspired swearing. The only other time I could remember was the time Dad's faithful old horse came uncorked one frosty morning and threw Dad all over the corral. John must have had a photographic memory, for he was using strange and weird sounding words the meaning of which escaped Felix and me (and John, too, for that matter).

John was all ready to go to school, but Peewee had different ideas. This may have been where the idea of

passive resistance developed. Peewee stood there, his
head drooping, his eyes half-closed. John tried everything he could think of to make a horse move. Peewee
was indifferent. He just stood. Finally Felix, who was
quite a sharp kid even if he was just four years old, took a
length of baling wire from the fence. He doubled it and
silently handed it to John. John brought it down over
Peewee's spotted rump. Slowly and sluggishly Peewee
started off down the road. Felix and I watched them until
they went over a little rise. As they went out of sight, we
could still see John's arm rising and falling rhythmically.

This little ordeal was repeated every morning, except
that John finally got so he could kick Peewee in the
stomach, tighten the cinch, swing up, and kick him in the
jaw all in one swift, fluid movement.

Felix and I stood by the corral fence to watch John
come home every afternoon. This was an entirely different story bearing no relationship to the way he started off
in the morning. The teacher eared Peewee down and held
on, while John wrapped the reins around the saddle horn
then wrapped his hands around the reins. When the
teacher was sure that John was set, she turned Peewee
loose. Peewee left for home in an ear-flattened run. Felix
and I first saw a little cloud of dust over the rise, then
Peewee burst over the hill like a comet, John hanging on
to the saddle horn with both hands and riding at a backward cant of about forty-five degrees. Peewee skidded up
to a halt at the barn door, his head dropping to his knees.
John's head fell over on his chest. They remained in this
position for a few minutes, looking for all the world like
the picture, *The End of the Trail*. Then John slid wearily off
Peewee's back, unsaddled him, and fed him.

John grew up that winter. His babyhood peeled off him like the shuck from an ear of corn. His mouth grew stern and thin lipped. Determination and willpower blossomed in his soul. He moved his bed out to the bunkhouse, where the other cowboys slept. From then on Peewee, John, and his baling wire were a part of the regular work force on the ranch.

That next summer, I decided I had better learn to ride. I had heard Dad making little hints that I, too, would be given a pony on my sixth birthday. In my childish mind I reasoned that this was something that should be prepared for in any way possible. I started practicing on Peewee.

I didn't bother with the saddle. I knew I could never go through the routine that John did. It was the work of only an hour or so to get the bridle on Peewee's head. Then I could not ride him away from the house. He just refused to go for me. But I figured it out. I got those bridle reins in a firm grasp and pulled Peewee down the road away from the house. It was no small task. I tugged and jerked and pulled and sweated. Peewee plodded along behind me, moving each foot with the slowness of a person mounting the thirteen steps.

When I had towed him as far as my strength lasted, I put the bridle reins over his neck, grabbed a handful of mane, and made a wild leap as Peewee whirled and started for the house. I learned to get on Peewee from almost any angle and at almost every speed.

This practice stood me in good stead later that summer. On the morning of my sixth birthday, a pickup rattled up to the ranch and backed up to the loading chute. Mr. Harris led my pony down the ramp. It was love at first sight on my part. My pony was as black as my hair. There was not a bit of white on him. He was somewhat larger than Peewee and was sleek and fat.

Dad said, "Well, there he is, LaVerne. What are you going to name him?" I was too dazed with the pony's beauty to be able to answer.

Then Mr. Harris spoke. "LaVerne, you can name him anything you want to, but I really do wish that you would name him after me. You could call him Baldy." And Mr. Harris raised his hat to show me his bald head.

Mr. Harris owned the ranch that joined us on the south, and he had raised Baldy. I still do not know if Baldy was a gift from Mr. Harris or if my father bought him.

I nodded assent, and the pony became Baldy from that moment on. I did have a hard time for the next ten years explaining why my horse was named Baldy when he was solid black. Most horses named Baldy have white stripes down their faces.

Mr. Harris gave me the bridle reins, and Dad picked me up and set me up on Baldy. Then started my liberal education in the care and feeding of a Shetland pony. Like all Shetlands, Baldy was not above trying to bite a chunk out of any kid that was stupid enough to approach him without due caution. He, too, would bite at my leg as I got on, but he never learned Peewee's trick of blowing himself up. Rather, Baldy relied on the clamped-teeth method. I finally learned the lower jaw grasp that forces a horse to open his mouth. I pried Baldy's mouth open, jammed the bit between his teeth, then hurriedly jerked away my hand before he clipped off any fingers.

My brother Felix has always been the thoughtful type. He spent two years watching us two older children struggling with our ponies. When his sixth birthday approached and it seemed from certain conversations around the house that he was also going to get a pony, he grew more and more thoughtful.

He approached Dad. "Say, Dad, why don't you just give me old Spot? He's my kind of horse, and I think I'm his kind of boy, and I'd just a whole lot rather have old Spot than anything in the world."

Dad grinned and said, "Well, son, if you and Spot have reached an understanding, I wouldn't want to come between you. He's yours."

Spot was an ancient and amiable cow pony that had been retired from active service on the ranch for a year. He stood seventeen hands high. Felix got on him by the simple method of shinnying up his right front leg as if he were climbing a flagpole. Old Spot never even twitched. If John or I had tried that trick with our ponies we wouldn't have been able to sit down for weeks.

Dad died before my two younger sisters were very old, but Mother continued the tradition of a gift of a Shetland pony on a child's sixth birthday. Virginia was next in line. She was sentenced early to be the companion of a little bay-and-white skinful of treachery named Jack. My sister Barbara was handed over to Tennessee. Tennessee was a little hag of a mare, gray about the face, swaybacked and potbellied. She was not much larger than a St. Bernard dog and every bit as agile. Her great trick was crawling under fences. It did not matter a bit to her whether Barbara was on her at the time or not.

Shetland ponies never wear out. They are handed down from child to child. When John went away to college, Peewee was sold to Jim Hopson south of Clayton.

There he took over the care and training of Harry and Hal. Peewee died on Jim's ranch at the age of twenty-seven.

When my sister Virginia went into nurses' training, Jack became the property of Jimmy Pat Doherty. Jack lived to be thirty-two, and that is old, very old, even for a Shetland. I sold Baldy to a family of children in Colorado. Tennessee, who was very old when we got her, went back to the Harris Ranch to die in happy retirement at the age of twenty-eight.

Fred Claflin not only taught us how to avoid death at the teeth and hooves of our ponies, he also taught us how to swim. We learned in the small horse tank, really no larger than a trough and hardly bigger than a bathtub. Not even Fred knew about our swimming in the big storage tank. We probably should have told him, because he might have persuaded Dad to take that lid off.

Dad doted on his children, but he was always busy trading and politicking. Mother developed a horror of guns the time Dad decided to teach her to shoot. He took her out to the irrigation ditch where he had set up bottles and cans for targets. He explained the revolver to her, and Mother, following directions, squeezed off a couple of rounds. But when she pulled the trigger the third time the gun didn't fire. Mother tipped the pistol barrel toward her saying, "What's the matter with this thing?" She pulled the trigger again and the bullet went right past her nose, clipping a lock of hair on her forehead as it went by.

We kids were transfixed with horror as we realized Mother had narrowly missed shooting her face off, but Dad went berserk. He grabbed the gun from Mother's hand and stuck it under the seat of the car. He was swearing, almost screaming with rage at Mother for giving him such a fright. Then he punched out a fence post. Dad was never one to conceal his feelings.

After that experience there was no way either of our parents would have tried to teach us to shoot. The job fell to Fred. We learned with a little single-shot twenty-two. We learned well that all guns were always loaded and that Fred would banish us from his sight if we even thought of any kind of horseplay or foolery when we were in the presence of guns. John, Felix, and I all became crack shots with a rifle. How good I actually was I didn't realize until an incident that happened when my son Kelly was a little boy. He and I were going hunting. I was carrying a thirty-thirty and Kelly had the same little twenty-two I had learned to shoot with. We were walking toward the big hill when suddenly Kelly screamed, a sound that alerted me to mortal danger.

Kelly loves to tell this story: "When I screamed, Mama whirled around, jacked a shell into the barrel as she turned. Then she hipshot that tarantula." I felt silly, having gunned down a spider with a thirty-thirty rifle, but Kelly was only six and he had screamed so very loud. At any rate he was proud of me, and I like to think Fred would have been proud of my reflexes, if not of my overkill of a harmless though scary tarantula.

We followed Fred and the other cowboys as they went about their chores. They taught us such useful things as how to sharpen a pocketknife and how to use a ramrod to clean a gun. Fred showed us how to hold a deck of cards to fan out a gambler's rose and how to play solitaire. He also told us that we could never get lost if we always carried a deck of cards with us.

"How come, Fred? Why won't we get lost if we carry a

deck of cards with us?''

"Well, if you think you might be lost, just sit down and deal a hand of solitaire. Pretty soon someone will come up and look over your shoulder and tell you to play the red ten on the black jack. Then you just ask him where you are."

John was already school age when we came to the Valley. He had a horse and saddle and was able to do chores like bringing in the milk cows and the saddle horses. Then, too, John was the oldest son and had a different status than us younger kids. Sometimes he got to go with Dad on business trips to Clayton or Trinidad, and once he accompanied Dad and Mother to the Fat Stock Show in Denver. John was an associate cowboy, not an apprentice.

The two little girls, Virginia and Barbara, were several years younger than the rest of us and were already in another generation. They missed the cowboy experience almost entirely. I couldn't actually live with the cowboys as the two boys did. Fred took Felix to the bunkhouse when Felix was three and kept him by his side as near as possible for the next ten years. I tagged along as much as I could. Felix and I watched the cowboys shoe horses and repair the leather on bridles and saddles. We saw how they oiled the harnesses for the teams with neat's-foot oil and saddle soap. Sometimes we were graciously allowed to help. Occasionally we were permitted to work the bellows for the small forge where the men made horseshoes, tools, buckles, and hinges.

Felix was the wood carrier and fire builder for the bunkhouse. Once a meteor thundered across the sky above the Valley. Felix was on his way to the bunkhouse with firewood. I used his description of this incident in a poem.

For Felix E. Goodson, Jr.
(my brother, who told me this)

At eight he was privileged
by the cowboys
to bring in wood and build the fire.

In dark,
arms full of cedar,
he was between the woodpile
and the bunkhouse door.

The meteor drilled a hole
through burning air.

The light unshadowed every stone and weed.
Horses flared red nostrils.
A cow stood frozen,
head cocked to the east.

The mesa, alfalfa fields,
the river lined with trees,
a rabbit, all chiseled plain.

Then thunder, the path of smoke,
the shrieking of the hired girl.

The dark came back.

At eight, he saw a light
that etched the world in clear.
He saw the path,
and heard the thunder.

I meant for the poem to imply that this young boy had been inspired in a way that guided him through a strange and hazardous future, and perhaps there is a poetic truth in that thought.

But really, the cowboys and the cowboy country turned a seventeen-year-old into an incomparable survivor. Felix graduated from high school when he was fifteen and joined the army almost immediately. He lied about his age, of course, and Mother signed the papers. He was shipped to the Philippines in November of 1941 and was captured by the Japanese on Mindanao. Felix was on the prison ship that was bombed by the Americans. He escaped by swinging down the side of the ship on a rope. I'm sure Felix never thought of it at the time, but his experience climbing the cap rocks with bare toes and fingers must have helped in that long descent.

Swimming under the lid of the storage tank was essential training for his long swim to shore. Felix swam as quietly as possible, underwater as much as he could. He was, after all, an escaped prisoner, and the Japanese were all about and armed. Felix made it to shore and was actually free for a few days until a Japanese patrol picked him up.

For the three-and-one-half years that Felix was a prisoner of war, his main concern was food. His book *Sweet Salt* details his prisoner-of-war experience, and much of it was about the search for food. When we were children we also foraged any way we could. When I was in Arkansas, in that lush, fruitful land, I kept thinking of the treasures we could have found under the fruit, pecan, and walnut trees. I wrote this poem about searching for food.

Foraging

A child, desert born, soon learns
to hunt for food,
not that there wasn't food enough—
beef and beans and such—
but our mouths were wild for taste.
So in the spring we searched
in low sinks after rain
where Russian thistle grew
green slender needles.

We grazed those sinks
in wary truce with starving cows
thin after a long winter.

Every seven years
the piñons throw their cones
heavy with tiny nuts.
We robbed the desert rats for these,
wrecking their burrows
for nuts so sweet
we chewed them hull and all
straining out the bits of shell
between our teeth.

We fought the cactus
for the scarlet prickly pears,
leaning over
to reach among the spines
to grasp the thorny fruit.

We rubbed the pears with dirt
to rid them of the fine sharp barbs.
We never got them all.
Our lips and tongues grew sore and swollen,
stained with the blood-red juice.

Now in my yard in Arkansas
before my white frame house
the leaves are pebbled
with fat pecans,
and in the back
persimmons lie,
fermenting golden wine
for drunken wasps and butterflies.
A miracle of waste for one
who foraged once in desert.

Felix and his fellow prisoners ate anything they could find, insects and earthworms and one red-letter day an unwary cat they boiled in the sterilizer.

Our gleanings in the barren arroyos of New Mexico taught us a simple system of classification: edible and inedible. Even now I automatically assess my world for food. Today I saw some dandelions growing. They will make a fine salad.

Chapter 5

Company's Coming

Dad had many and various ways of getting under Mother's skin, but nothing could make her angrier than for him to say, "Okay, Stella. Send the kids out to the yard to gather up the silverware. Company's coming." Of course, it was true. We did take the knives and spoons out into the yard to play with, and we left them there. Mother hated to use tableware that had been out in the yard. She didn't like at all for Dad to remind her, and we did have lots of company.

We were terribly isolated. One might think if there were no large centers of population anywhere closer than Amarillo or Denver the world would hardly beat a path to our door, but it was the very isolation that brought company our way. After all, we did live on a genuine cattle ranch, and there were real cowboys and horses. Visitors came from Trinidad, from Amarillo, and by rail into Clayton from even more distant places. If men came to buy cattle or alfalfa seed they quite often brought their wives with them.

The twenties were strange years for the United States, full of contrast and anachronisms. The cities were wealthy and civilized. There were paved roads, in the towns anyway, and gorgeous automobiles. The women were stylish flappers with bobbed hair and knee-length dresses. They smelled wonderful.

When the visitors came down the dirt road off of Rief Hill into the Valley, the only sight that could have told them they were in the twentieth century was the telephone line.

The women in the Valley at least had the telephone. The brown oak boxes hung on their walls and the women were summoned to their phones with individual rings. Our ring was two longs and two shorts. We listened for our ring on a subconscious level and also automatically noted which of our neighbors was being called. There was a great deal of listening in, of course. One certainly did not expect to have any private conversations.

Once Mr. Jeffries from the bank at Trinidad had occasion to call Dad. It must have been a slack morning in the Valley, for there were so many listening in that Dad and Mr. Jeffries couldn't hear each other. Every receiver in use somehow caused a power drain.

Dad said, "Ladies, if you all will just hang up so I can hear Mr. Jeffries, I'll call you right back and tell you everything he said." Dad said the sound of the receivers going up was like thunder.

The telephone was such a marvel and so useful that it is no wonder a line was strung from Clayton to Kenton by the turn of the century. Another line came down the

Jessie and Will, November 1914. This rare photograph of an interior shows the vital telephone on the wall of a claim shack. (Center for Southwest Research, General Library, University of New Mexico, 992-018)

Valley from Trinidad in 1905. Ed Lord had the contract for cutting the poles and freighting them by team and wagon up and down the line.

It is a measure of the value of the telephone that only twenty-four years after its invention there were two lines coming into the Valley. It was a comfort in that isolated country to know that help with a problem or an exchange of friendly messages was at one's fingertips.

Although the women on the ranches had telephones like the women in the towns, there the similarity ended.

There were many differences between the lives of the women who came to visit and the women who lived in the Valley. Gas piped into the homes and electricity made most of the difference—gas and electricity, and, of course, plumbing.

Butane gas in bottles or tanks was not yet plentiful, so all the women in the Valley used wood stoves. Some had kerosene stoves for use in the summertime. Although a relief from the heat of the old cook stove, the kerosene stoves were treacherous. If a woman turned her back on one, it promptly went up in smoke. The greasiest black smoke imaginable hung festoons of soot all over the kitchen.

In the towns, women lighted their homes by the clicking of a switch. Women in the Valley struggled with a dangerous contrivance called an Aladdin lamp. The Aladdin lamp burned kerosene as did our regular lamps, but the Aladdin had a round wick and a mantle. The mantle hung over the wick, and both the mantle and wick had to be in perfect balance or the Aladdin lamp smoked like the kerosene stoves. The gradual darkening of the room was the first warning. Then someone would yell, "Get the lamp." The person nearest the lamp would make a wild lunge to turn it down.

The smoke an Aladdin lamp could put out was awesome. The mantle was a cone of gauze, actually the free-hanging ashes of a cone of gauze. The mantle came in a little box and was coated with some sort of flammable material. The mantle was suspended in a little metal framework that fit over the wick. Mother carefully placed the mantle over the wick, then set it afire with a match. After it was burned, the mantle was a totally unsubstan-

tial cone of ash. If it was touched it crumbled immediately, but it did give off a soft white light that was
infinitely brighter than that the ordinary kerosene lamps
could provide. However, if the mantle and wick were
even a hair off balance, soot would begin to form like a
black tumor on the side of the mantle. When the soot
caught fire, flame rushed up the chimney and smoke shot
out and eddied and curled about the ceiling. I see old
Aladdins now in antique shops, wired for electricity, of
course. They were beautiful, and every home had one or
two, but they didn't work worth a hoot.

Electricity meant refrigeration. Lack of it meant the
milk house and the cooling vats. Water flowed from the
overhead tank into a deep vat, a yard square and perhaps
two feet deep. From there the water flowed into a shallow
vat a yard wide and five feet long but only four inches
deep. The water ran from the shallow vat, by an overflow
pipe, into the big storage tank. The well water was cold.
The milk, cream, and butter that Mother placed in the shallow vat stayed sweet and usable for a couple of days at
least. Of course it was a real chore for Mother to trudge
back and forth to the milk house if she needed a cup of milk.

Gas and electricity, in those days, were unobtainable,
but plumbing was not. We could have had a bathroom
with the means available. The only power we needed was
gravity. I don't know why persons in those days didn't
exert more energy toward plumbing. I remember when
the men finally dug a trench across the yard, laid pipe,
and ran water into the kitchen. That must have seemed
all the luxury anyone could possibly need, and no one
thought of having a toilet indoors, or a bathtub. There
wouldn't have been any hot water, but a large kettle of

boiling water could take the chill off a tub of cold water. It would have been wonderful just to pull a plug instead of carrying dirty water back outside.

The visitors who came from that glamorous world of plumbing, electricity, and gas parked their cars by the hard-pan dirt yard. Mother always had a vegetable garden on the west side of the house, and there she also grew a few flowers, but she gave up on the front yard. If the expected company was very important, Dad sent one of the hands out to rake the yard—a chore they all hated.

Shorty Quimby bought the Roberts Ranch from the bank when we moved up on the Smylie place. Shorty and Kathryn Quimby tore down part of the house where we had lived and built a beautiful new home. Mrs. Quimby planted a lawn around her house. That lawn was a wonder to the Valley. It was the only lawn in the whole country then, and if it still survives is probably the only lawn there now. I can't even imagine the hard work that lawn must have cost Mrs. Quimby. The soil there was compacted by years of running by barefoot children. The yard had never been cultivated, nor had it ever had any plants in it. If it rained, the mud had the consistency of glue.

That mud furnished us with one of our favorite chores, cracking dirt balls off chickens' toes. As I remember it, the younger chickens got the worst dirt balls. We would see the poor little chickens slogging along with a ball three-quarters of an inch in diameter on each toe. They could hardly walk and were certainly no trouble to catch. We put their feet on one rock and gently pounded on the dirt ball with another. When we got all the dirt off we put the chickens on the ground and shooed them. Those chickens bounced around like popcorn. They were still exerting all the energy they had needed to move with dirt balls on their feet and, as a result, leaped a foot or two into the air at every step. We thought this was hilarious.

When Mrs. Quimby moved to the Roberts Ranch she solved the problem of that hard-pan yard by digging up the entire yard with a spade. She removed the dirt with a wheelbarrow and wheeled more soil in from the irrigation ditch. She went up to the mesas and loaded five-gallon buckets with humus from under the oak brush. She built up the front edge of the yard where it sloped toward the arroyo, and she smoothed and leveled and watered and planted. The lawn came up like an emerald island in that dry, dusty country.

The lawn was a great temptation to livestock. There was no buffer zone between the yard and the horse pasture. The horses and milk cows came and leaned on the fence and yearned toward that grass. One day when the Quimbys were gone, the horses leaned the latch loose on the gate, and in went the whole herd. They ate the lawn, then went around the house and ate all the flowers. They were just finishing off the iris bed when Mrs. Quimby came back home.

She grimly started over respading the yard and reseeding. Her lawn was once again glorious. The Quimbys went for a visit to Oklahoma, and while they were gone their beautiful home burned. The walls exploded out over the lawn and cooked it. The debris had hardly cooled before Mrs. Quimby rolled her wheelbarrow up and started clearing her lawn.

Mrs. Quimby's lawn and Stella Goodson's tablecloth, not to mention Aladdin lamps, have become to me symbols of the odds these two ranch women struggled against.

They both taught school, cooked for hands, cared for children and their husbands, washed and ironed and made gardens, but they found time for things as purely frivolous as a blue-grass lawn or a linen tablecloth.

In their homes in the cities the ladies who came to visit us had gas or electric cookstoves, but Mother prepared an enormous midday dinner on the old Home Comfort wood and coal range.

She spread her table with an Irish linen damask tablecloth, never mind the agony it had been to iron it with the sadirons. Dad had given Mother the tablecloth, and she prized it highly.

Mother ruined that cloth sometime after Dad died. Jiggs and John had killed a deer, and Mother reached into the dresser drawer for a sheet to wrap the fresh meat in. She mistakenly got the tablecloth and wrapped it around the meat for Jiggs to bring home. I did not realize that it was Mother's linen cloth until it was ruined with bloodstains. Mother managed to save a small square out of the tablecloth. She hemmed that square by hand, and I am so glad I have it. Not one stitch in that hem shows. Around the little cloth are four yards of perfect needlework.

The meals Mother set out on that tablecloth were as carefully constructed as the blind stitching in that hem. If it was summertime, and most of our company did arrive in the summer, the big platter held fried chicken. It is impossible to cook chicken like that today. You could find the huge iron skillets, but the wood stoves that heated those skillets evenly have vanished.

There was no refrigeration, so the meat we ate was seasonal. In the summer we had chicken, snatched fresh from the chicken yard. Dad butchered hogs in the fall and cured out ham and bacon. In the winter sides of beef went upon the north side of the barn. Actually we were fairly well supplied with beef at all times, because Dad butchered for some of the grocery stores in Clayton. He always saved out choice cuts for the house.

Mother's company meals were not much different from those she put on the table for her husband, children, and the hands. Perhaps she got up early to bake a cake for company, and maybe if the visitors got lucky the cake would have Mother's lemon icing on it. Mother was in her eighties when I tried to get her to tell me how she made that wonderful clear, golden icing, and she said she used butter, egg yolks, sugar, and lemon juice and cooked it in an iron skillet, but she could not tell me the proportions.

I have been tempted to experiment to see if I could retrieve that recipe, but I'm afraid the icing might turn out like the noodles. Mother always made her own egg noodles. I had watched her so often that I was sure I could do it. I mixed the egg yolks into the flour along with salt and baking powder. (That may have been my mistake. I probably should not have used baking powder. But what? I don't know.) I rolled the dough out as thin as I could and then rolled the sheet of dough into a tube. I cut the noodles carefully and shook them out, just as Mother did. I left them to dry, perhaps not long enough. Then I brought my pot of chicken broth to a boil and carefully dropped a double handful of noodles into the boiling pot. The reaction was so immediate and so unexpected that I stood shrieking into my pot of noodles as they swelled and twisted and writhed. Those noodles looked completely alive and utterly loathsome. They were also as tough as whet leather.

I gave up trying to remember how Mother cooked things. I knew I would never be able to make hominy as she did, in a five-gallon crock. She soaked the dry corn in water to which she had added a little lye. Then she washed and washed the corn, letting water run through, taking the hulls and lye with it.

Mother cooked all the time. The late twenties were affluent years with plenty of rain for crops and gardens. Those are the years the company came. What made a company dinner special was, of course, the tablecloth. Mother lofted that gleaming white cloth and sent it billowing out over the old round table, which had become oval and enormous with three added leaves.

That tablecloth caused Mother—and me, too—some considerable embarrassment. We had extra grand company this time, two men in dark suits and high white collars as elegant as Arrow shirt ads. They were bankers, I think, from some city in the East.

It was a convention that women were invisible as they went about their cooking. Their faces were flushed, perhaps their hair was awry, and they had on aprons. So one just did not see them until they took their aprons off and powdered their noses.

The two elegant men and Dad were sitting in the living room. Mother realized that her tablecloth was in the chest against the living-room wall. She depended on being invisible as she slipped into the room and headed for the chest. The minute she set foot in the room the two guests snapped to their feet. Dad, seeing his guests shoot upright, also jumped to his feet and looked wildly around for danger. Mother sketched a little bow and backed into the kitchen. The men all sat down again.

Mother was really distressed. Her dinner was ready, she wanted to set the table, and she needed her tablecloth. She went to the kitchen door and called me in from the yard. "LaVerne, just slip into the living room and get my tablecloth out of the bottom drawer in the chest. Go through the front door."

I ran around the house and stepped into the living room from the front. The two elegant men saw me and once again leaped to their feet. Once again, Dad looked around in alarm and jumped up. I looked up and saw all those men looming over me, looking at me, and fled into the yard. I went back to the kitchen door. "Mother, Dad and those men jumped up and looked at me. They scared me."

Mother dropped her head into her hands and I could see her shoulders shaking. I thought she was crying but soon realized she was convulsed with laughter. "It's all right, LaVerne. I'll get the cloth."

Mother stepped swiftly into the living room and said sternly, "Gentlemen, remain seated. I'll just be a moment."

In the spring of 1928, the sick young rich man came to the ranch. His visit had been arranged through the banks. The banker in Battle Creek, Michigan, had written the bank in Trinidad, Colorado, to ask if they could find a place on a ranch for the young man to stay awhile. Mr. Jeffries called Dad and made the arrangements. I cannot remember the young man's name and neither could my older brother, John, but it seems that it might have been Charles. I wish I could remember his last name, for it was a famous one. He was a son of one of the great food-processing families in Battle Creek. I simply am not able to recall which family, but Fred showed us Charles's last name on a box of some sort of food, and told us that Charles was rich.

I don't know what was wrong with Charles's health, but he was very pale. I had never seen a pale man before. Even Dad, who spent all his time in the shelter of his car, was sun and wind burned, and the cowboys were the color of old saddles.

Charles arrived in Clayton by train, and Dad went in and brought him out. Charles was a big man, nineteen years old. He brought a lot of luggage with him, some of it being long tubes of candy.

Charles moved into the bunkhouse with the cowboys and went out to work with them every morning. However, after the noon meal Charles went to the bunkhouse and took a nap. We children were under strict orders to be quiet, but as soon as he waked up Felix and I, and sometimes John, were waiting for him. Of course we were interested in the candy. We must have stared at him big-eyed and wistful until he brought out a tube of candy, unscrewed the top, and passed out a piece or two to each of us.

I later called John to ask him if he remembered the young man, and he recalled him clearly. Like me, he couldn't remember Charles's actual name, but like me, John clearly recalled the candy. He also told me that Charles had shipped a bale of Dad's choice alfalfa hay back to Battle Creek to see if it could be used in the manufacture of candy. I don't think anything ever came of it.

Before he left, Charles went up to Santa Fe and Taos to see the sights of New Mexico, and he brought back presents. I don't remember what he brought Mother, but he brought me a little leather case with Indian designs on it and a comb and mirror inside. He brought Virginia a silver and turquoise ring. I must have pointed like a hunting dog when I saw that ring. The only rings I had ever seen were Mother's wedding ring and Dad's Masonic Lodge ring, but I didn't think of them as jewelry. They were just part of Mother's and Dad's hands. This ring, however, was jewelry and small enough for a child's hand, and I wanted it.

Mother said, "LaVerne, Virginia is only two years old and won't be able to wear that ring for several years. If Charles doesn't mind, maybe you could wear the ring now and save it for Virginia." I looked up at Charles in wild hope, and he smiled and handed me the ring.

I lost it, of course. Mother rented a house and moved to Clayton to await the birth of Barbara, her last child. A woman came to stay with her and help look after Virginia and Felix and me. This woman took us to the movies one night. It was the first movie I had ever seen, and it seemed perfectly real to me. The hero and a girl were dashing madly across the prairie in a wagon, being pursued by Indians. In my anxiety I was twisting the ring on my finger. The ring came off and dropped to the floor of the theater and rolled away.

I went into immediate hysterics and the poor woman had to drag me, kicking and screaming, from the theater. She did get me quiet long enough to ask the theater manager to look out for the ring, but of course it was lost forever.

I often think of that young man and wonder how he fared. He would be in his eighties now if he is still alive. I have wondered how he viewed his stay on a ranch in New Mexico. I imagine that he learned to appreciate plumbing and central heat and a private bedroom. I hope he did. He was a brave young man to come so far from home, alone and ill, to live in a crowded bunkhouse with a bunch of unwashed cowboys.

Dad was the manager of the Roberts Ranch. It belonged by reason of foreclosure to the First National Bank of Trinidad. It was for sale all the time we lived there, and that was the reason we had so many bankers to visit us. The Roberts Ranch was a large and valuable one. It had approximately seven thousand acres of grazing land, one hundred acres of dry-land farming, and five hundred acres of alfalfa under irrigation. In those boom days of the late twenties the ranch was a good investment, and so the bankers and other investors came to appraise it for purchase.

Once a year, in the fall, the hunters came. They came for the deer that fattened on the alfalfa and grainfields at night. These were legal hunters, not to be confused with Jiggs Collins and peers.

Ted Hanna came every year. He owned a grocery store in Amarillo and brought wonderful, exotic food with him. We children would have traded Dad's fine beefsteaks all day long for Ted Hanna's bologna and would have given up Mother's wonderful home-baked bread for a loaf of sliced white bread. There were doughnuts and cupcakes and candy, lots of candy. Ted brought jelly and pickles, dates and raisins, apples and oranges and bananas. Two or three other hunters always accompanied Ted. Hunting season was full of excitement. I woke up while it was still dark. I could smell bacon and coffee and could hear the men milling around in the kitchen. Mother never cooked breakfast for the hunters.

It was part of the hunting mystique of these city men that they should cook their breakfast on an old wood stove and pack a saddlebag lunch of biscuits and bacon. At first light the cowboys brought up the horses, the hunters mounted up, and their western day began. The cowboys went along mainly to see that none of the visitors accidentally shot a cow. Dad never went with them. I don't know what excuse he gave, but actually Dad hated to ride a horse. He felt that if he couldn't get somewhere in his Model A he didn't need to go.

He was always at hand to greet the brave hunters as they came crippling in. They seemed to revive a bit after a huge supper cooked by Mother.

I have no idea where they slept. Maybe they crowded into the bunkhouse with their bedrolls, or perhaps they bedded down in the hay barn. Neither do I have any idea why the hunters put themselves through such an ordeal year after year. Although they quite often got a deer, at the time I could not imagine why they worked so hard for deer meat when they had all that lovely bologna.

Another visitor came to the ranch, and of all the visitors, to me, was the most magical. Her name was Reba McCormic.

I remember a beautiful red-haired girl up on a great golden stallion. The horse's name was Sundown, and he waltzed and pranced sideways just as if he knew he was carrying the daughter of a princess.

There were five of us: my two brothers and me, one of the cowboys, and that beautiful woman. My older brother, John, and the cowboy, Punch, were riding full-sized horses, but my younger brother, Felix, and I were riding Shetland ponies. I vaguely wished I could have been up on a real horse so I could have ridden stirrup to stirrup with the girl, but it hardly mattered. I was so dazzled that every plant and stone seemed to glow and even the rim of the Black Mesa was outlined with golden sparkles.

I was eleven, and curiosity and boredom had driven me through hundreds of books. I had my own definitions of royalty, my own heraldry. I half suspected I was, myself, a princess, lost somehow in this arid, isolated northeast corner of New Mexico.

Mother whispered about the girl, and of course I heard the whispers. No one could keep anything from me. At night I drifted like a wraith from room to room and, indeed, around the whole ranch area.

Mother's whispers said, "Of course, she's Reba Rankin. Don't I know? I grew up with Mamie in Arkansas. She was a little older, but I remember when she married that redheaded Joe Rankin and this little red-haired girl was born." My dad grunted and turned over. He was uncomfortable in the bed where my little sisters usually slept. My sisters had been shoved into my room on a pallet on the floor. In the custom of that time, any guest was an honored one and was given the best bed.

I had followed Mother around the house while she was getting the room ready. I was amazed at how thorough she was. Mother took her own things away from the dresser drawers and the old brown wardrobe. She relined the drawers with newspaper, and from the top shelf of the wardrobe took one of her finest pieces of fancywork, an embroidered dresser scarf with an edging of tatting four inches deep. She put fresh ironed sheets and one of Granny's quilts on the bed, and most wonderful of all, spread over the bed my great-grandmother's hand-spun counterpane. All these preparations made me more sure than ever that we were entertaining royalty.

I know now that Mother was setting out the best she had for the daughter of an old neighbor from Arkansas. The neighbor's name was Mamie Harris. She was born in Belleville, Arkansas, in 1886. She married the redheaded Joe Rankin and had a red-haired daughter. She left Arkansas, divorced Joe Rankin, took another name, and became a soprano with a great opera company. She toured Europe and the United States and married and divorced a prince.

It was this last fact that established firmly in my eleven-year-old head that we were receiving a visit from a princess. Our guest's name was Reba. She was the granddaughter of Old Man Harris, the rancher to the south of us. He had brought Reba over for an overnight visit.

When Mr. Harris and Reba came through the door, Mother said, "Now, your name is Rankin, isn't it?"

The girl stiffened. "Oh, no," she said. "My mother is Mary McCormic."

Mother turned to my dad and said, "Felix, this is Reba McCormic."

It was this incident that occasioned Mother's whispers in the night. I could tell that Mother was miffed because Reba didn't bear her father's name.

Reba was a gracious person. Mother showed her to the room, put the lamp down, and said good night. I stayed in the doorway, and Reba smiled at me and asked me to come in. I sidled in, absolutely tongue-tied. I watched while Reba took clothes from the suitcase and hung them. Then she brushed her hair and did things to her face. I think I spoke for the first time when she took her earrings from her ears. "You've got holes in your ears," I blurted.

"Oh, yes, that way I won't lose my earrings." I nodded, thinking of all the fabulous jewels that any princess would have to guard against losing. It was the first time I had ever seen pierced ears.

Reba reached into her purse and took out a tiny flashlight. "Now, will you walk outside with me?" When we got to the door of the outhouse, she turned and said, "If you'll watch that no one comes, I'll watch for you."

It seems bizarre to me now to think of that grubby, stringy-haired, skinny little kid standing rigid as a tree stump beside an outhouse, firmly convinced that she was guarding a princess.

I don't remember breakfast the next morning, but I recall the saddling up. The whole family was there, along with three cowboys. I realized why I was permitted to go. I was a sort of chaperone. My mother didn't ride, and I was the only other female available. It was of course unthinkable that we would send a young lady off in the company of men only. We were careful about those things back in 1932.

I remember now why Reba came to the ranch. She came to buy the horse. That was the purpose of the ride, so she could try him out. That was why the cowboy came along. The horse was high spirited, and there was a discussion as to whether Reba could handle him.

After Reba left that afternoon, I aggravated some of the story out of Mother. Mother was born in Yell County, Arkansas. Her family traded with Old Man Harris, who ran a country store there. He had two sons and a girl named Mamie. Mamie had a glorious voice and, Mother said, wanted to do something with her voice, her life. She married and had a little girl. Then she left, Mother said, left Arkansas, and that was all Mother knew. Mother and

Dad were shopping in Kenton when Mother met Mr. Harris again. She recognized him and learned that he had bought a ranch just south of us.

Mother asked about Mamie, and he told her that Mamie was an opera singer in Chicago and had changed her name to Mary McCormic. Over the years we heard bits and pieces of news about Mary McCormic. One night we all gathered around the old battery radio to hear her sing. Mr. Harris had let us know she would be on a program.

My mother had known and still remembered Mamie Harris. I shall never forget the ride with her daughter that long-ago morning in New Mexico, and there are still a few who remember Mary McCormic.

I found a few terse entries in *Who's Who*, such as the one for 1928:

McCormic, Mary (Stage Name) Singer b Belleville, ARK; studied music at Northwestern Univ. Sang in choir at Northwestern U Chicago; became protege of Mary Garden; debut as "Michaela" in Carmen with Mary Garden Nov. 26, 1921; Italian debut as "Santuzza" in Cavelliera Rusticana in opera house at Asti, 1922; formerly mem. Chicago Civic Opera Co. *(Who's Who 1928)*

I located an obituary at last in *Opera*, May, 1981:

Obit. *Opera* My '81 32:471

Mary McCormic

American soprano in Amarillo, Texas, on Feb. 10, Aged 95. She was born in Belleville, and was a protege of Mary Garden with whom she studied. She made her debut in Chicago as Michaela with Garden in Carmen. After three seasons in Chicago, she went to Italy for further study. In 1936 she made her debut as Juliet to the Romeo of Georges Thill and was also heard as Marguerite and Salome in

Herodiade. In 1929 she went to the Opera Comique, where her roles included Manon, Louise, Mimi, and Cio-Cio-San. She sang with the San Carlos Touring Opera in the mid-1930s, and after 1939 returned permanently to America appearing with Bing Crosby in broadcasts and in a film with Janet Gaynor. In 1944 she settled in Denton where she founded the first university opera workshop in the Southwest at North Texas State College. She recorded duets from Manon with Thill on Columbia.

I was shocked to see her death date. I had no idea she had lived so long. I was also shocked by the lack of any personal data. Mary McCormic appeared to have existed only in her work. Of course, that was the way of it. When Mary McCormic came on stage, Mamie Harris vanished.

I called several music historians and professors of music, but none had ever heard of Mary McCormic. So I realized that Mary McCormic had also vanished. I decided that should not happen. I wanted so much to bring her back. She was important to all of us in the Cimarron Valley—a tenuous connection to an outside world of stardom and glamor. Also, she was the daughter of Old Man Harris and the sister of O'Dell Harris, our own outrageous folk hero. In fact, to us all I am sure O'Dell's ride to the top of the Herring Hotel overshadowed any other accomplishment of the Harris family.

Almost everyone who knew about Mary McCormic is now dead, but Marion Collins, my two brothers, and I still remember her and her beautiful daughter. I am delighted to pay a tribute to Reba McCormic because she was gracious to me and gave me a glimpse of a world of face creams, beautiful clothes, and jeweled earrings. She made a difference in my life.

Chapter 6

Civilizing the Children

I don't know what finally alerted the parents of the Valley, but at some point they realized they had a bunch of half-grown barbarians for children. It may have been the episode of the skunk that convinced the parents that we children were in need of a major cultural change.

Jiggs Collins and Jack Rutledge were two or three years older than John, my oldest brother. The two older boys persuaded John to act as a point man in a skunk roundup. Actually it was just one skunk, but one skunk is a gracious plenty in any given situation.

A skunk was a valuable fur animal, but as the boys had no traps or guns they decided to capture this skunk with their bare hands. It was night, but the moon was shining. They could see the skunk ambling down an arroyo, so Jiggs told John to run up ahead and turn the skunk back toward

Jack and him. John obediently trotted off down the bank of the arroyo, got ahead of the skunk, and slid down the bank in front of it. The skunk lumbered toward John, and he jumped in front of it, waving his arms to turn it back.

The skunk turned, lifted his tail, and sprayed John right in the face. John fell to the ground retching and gagging, and the skunk ambled on past him down the arroyo. Jiggs and Jack helped John to the house. Jiggs and Jack were tainted, but John was completely saturated with skunk odor.

Dad heated water for John to bathe in and put the tub of water out by the alfalfa field. Beside the tub Mother placed her barber shears and some clean old clothes. John was pointed toward the tub and directed to cut off all his hair and then to scour thoroughly. Dad poured gasoline on John's stinking clothes and burned them. Then he fixed John a bed in a wagon that the men pushed off toward the arroyo. Those cowboys certainly were not going to let John back into the bunkhouse. He wandered about the ranch, a pariah for several days. Mother fed him outside and supplied him with reading materials until he could rejoin the family.

Dad's tolerance for personal inconvenience was real low. His anger over the skunk was almost as bad as when we gave him the itch. Scabies was epidemic in the Valley. John had been to stay overnight with some neighbor or other. He came home with the itch, and before Mother knew what was happening all of us had it. Even Dad. His wrath was majestic. He issued a royal decree that any kid of his had better goddamn well not ask to stay all night anywhere ever, and they goddamn well better not ask for anyone to stay over at home!

The cure for itch was heroic. Mother smeared us all with lard in which she had mixed sulphur. All our clothes and all our bedding had to be boiled.

When George Wiggins's kids got scabies, George took the old motor washing machine out to the pasture, filled it with gasoline, and washed all his kids' clothes and shoes. This appallingly dangerous procedure worked. The sulphur and lard worked too, but any ointment capable of killing the scabies parasites burned and stunk and made hair look really weird.

In those days scabies was a disgrace, equated with filth, poverty, general shiftlessness, and loss of the hope of heaven. When Reva Rae, the dainty, beloved only child of Shorty and Kathryn Quimby, got scabies, Mrs. Quimby didn't have the foggiest idea what was wrong. She tried washes and powders, and of course they didn't work. Reva Rae's back became a mass of lesions. Shorty drove her to Trinidad to the doctor. The diagnosis of scabies horrified the Quimbys, and it's likely they would never have mentioned it to anyone, for nobody ever did mention such a thing. Not so Reva Rae. She had unusually clear diction for a three year old, and evidently a photographic memory. There was a gathering at our house, and someone asked Reva Rae how she was.

Her clear voice floated out over the room. "Daddy took me to the doctor in Trinidad." Mrs. Quimby's head snapped up. The clear voice continued, "And the doctor said I had the itch." That ended the conspiracy of silence about scabies, because after they quit laughing Mother and everyone else besieged Mrs. Quimby to tell what the doctor had said and what sort of cure he had prescribed.

Because she was the teacher, I have never been able

to call her anything but Mrs. Quimby. She was younger than my mother or Marion (Mrs. Collins) or Mrs. Rutledge and perhaps more knowledgeable of the world, even though she did not know much about the itch. She was only a few years out of college, while Mrs. Rutledge and Mother had been out of school for many years.

Mrs. Quimby was teaching the older children of both school districts while Mother taught the elementary grades. Mrs. Quimby had decided on her own that her students could use a little civilizing. She organized a school banquet. All of us had serviceable table manners. We did not eat with our hands or make rude noises at the table, but Kathryn Quimby introduced us to a different set of manners. The banquet was at her house. Jack Rutledge, Everett Like, Peggy Davis, Jimmy Wiggins, Laura Gay Quigg, Velna Behimer, and my brother John and I were those I remember being there, although I am not certain about Jack Rutledge and Velna Behimer.

The table was set with matching china and silver and a lace tablecloth. There were candles and a flower centerpiece and white linen napkins. There was a small glass of tomato juice at each plate. Mrs. Quimby herself waited on us, and when she told us to begin, we picked up that tomato juice as one person and knocked it back in one swallow. We then sat there waiting happily for whatever delights might be given us.

I was sitting next to Jimmy Wiggins. In his nervousness he kept tilting back on the back legs of his chair. I didn't know much, but I did know this wasn't proper behavior. When Jimmy brought the chair forward so he could get a bite to eat, I placed my right foot firmly on his chair rung. Every time Jimmy tried to lean back I brought him forward. This struggle went on through the salad (served on its own plate, a wonder to us all) and the chicken with dressing, and continued through the dessert. I don't think Jimmy had any idea that I was the cause of the strange behavior of his chair. He was bewildered and I was exhausted.

Whatever the flash point, the parents of the Valley decided to do something about the state of their children's savagery. Our lives began to change.

We were not complete savages. We went to church and to school activities and to the traveling movies shown at times in Kenton. These were passive activities, however, and required nothing of us by way of interaction with others. Everyone agreed that the young of the Valley needed a way to associate with each other short of rounding up skunks in the moonlight.

Mother, Ada Behimer, Mrs. Rutledge, and several of the ladies at Kenton organized a dance club. This club was for all of us between the ages of twelve and eighteen. If there was a child of the right age, the whole family was included.

Reva Rae was only five at the time, but it was unthinkable that we would have any function whatever that did not include Mrs. Quimby. She came aboard as an advisor.

June Quigg was the fashion expert. She and her husband Ed, with their thirteen-year-old daughter, came to the Valley in the early thirties at the depth of the Great Depression and drought. They went to work for George Wiggins. June was a pretty woman, feminine and frilly. She wore makeup and perfume, ruffles and bows, and did her hair. Of course, other women in the Valley, Kathryn

Quimby and Catharine Sumpter, for example, were always nicely turned out, and Mother always looked fine
when she went out in public, but the Valley was used to
them. June, however, put on makeup every morning and
curled her hair every night. June Quigg was like an exotic
bird alighting in a chicken yard. Mother went to Trinidad
for a permanent and came back with curly hair, rouge,
lipstick, and powder.

June undertook the task of getting us girls dressed for
our first dance. The boys weren't that much trouble, it
having been decided that their church-going garb was
just fine. No parent in the Valley was foolish enough to
put a growing boy into a suit. The boys dressed in white
shirts, ties, dress pants, and V-necked sweaters.

We, however, had long dresses. And hose, and high-
heeled shoes, and even bras. Only one or two of us really
needed a bra, but we were allowed to have them, so we all
strapped ourselves in, flat chested or not.

I had two new dresses. June sewed up the side seams
on two dresses my aunt Mary had sent. Aunt Mary was six
feet tall, so her street dresses came to the floor on me. I
don't expect they could have stood much of an inspec-
tion, but the dresses weren't going to appear in any bright
lights, and I loved them. One was a light orange dimity
with white lines running through it, and the other was
navy blue dotted swiss trimmed in white.

Mother contributed her long green dress for Peggy
Davis, and all the other girls in the Valley had new dresses
or made ones, something frilly anyway, and long. We all
envisioned being whirled in graceful circles with our
long, long dresses swirling about our high-heeled feet.

Peggy was living with us at the time, and Dad took us

both to Clayton for high-heeled shoes. I don't think Mother and Grace Davis were too happy with the shoes we picked out. They were multicolored suede sandals with ankle straps and four-inch heels. I don't know why at least one of us didn't break an ankle. We staggered around holding on to the backs of chairs. It took a surprisingly short time for us to learn how to walk without active disgrace, however, and as I remember, for all we were gawky adolescents, the girls of the Valley were graceful and pretty in their new long dresses and high-heeled shoes.

Of course none of us could dance, so Shorty volunteered to help teach us. Dad said he was the waltz king of the West and he also would teach us. June and Ed were of great help. They had come from Missouri and knew some of the old folk dances—the schottische, the heel-and-toe, and a dance we called, "Put your little foot."

We began to practice at our house. We cranked up the old Victrola, and June and Ed, Dad and Shorty pulled and pushed us around. Peggy, Laura Gay, and I were instructed by the men, and June taught the boys: Jack Rutledge, John, and others who sometimes wandered by. Then we were ordered to dance with each other. We could have been embarrassed, but we were so anxious to master this new skill that we grimly held on to each other and circled the floor. John and Jack could both play the harmonica, so they took turns playing the folk dances so we could practice them.

There were great goings on in the Valley. We were all learning so many new things that we were giddy with excitement. We were eager to embrace any new knowledge, including novel aspects of personal hygiene.

June introduced the girls to Mum, and the girls introduced themselves to Tangee lipstick and Evening in Paris
perfume, not to mention Blue Waltz. Tangee lipstick
came in tiny brass tubes, samples I suppose. It was both
waxy and greasy and was bright orange in color. The
selling point for Tangee lipstick was that the one color
was all that was needed because it turned color to suit the
person wearing it. It did turn bright pink on the lips,
although it didn't seem to look much different on Laura
Gay, who was blonde, than it did on me, whose hair was
coal black. Tangee sold for a dime for the little tube. There
may have been large tubes that sold for more, but I don't
remember ever seeing any. I have often wondered what
chemicals we were smearing on our lips.

Evening in Paris perfume came in cobalt blue bottles
sold separately or in large silver presentation cases. The
bottles nestled in little sinks of silver satin and contained
perfume, cologne, and something called toilet water. We
all wanted one of those cases. Actually we wanted some
young man to give us one, a silver box of Evening in Paris
being tantamount to a declaration. I still see the bottles in
antique stores and always, just for a moment, I am overcome by longing.

We happily lacerated our armpits and flayed our legs
with Gillette safety razors. Those heavy metal razors of
the thirties were not like the razors today. The word
"safety" meant only that the razors could not be used to
commit murder. They certainly would excoriate human
flesh unless used with great care.

The rules of the dance club were fairly simple. One
couldn't belong to the club and go to public dances. I
believe one of the reasons for our parents' organizing the

club was to institute that rule. The public dances held at some ranch homes, and in public buildings in some of the little towns up on top, were forbidden to most of us. These dances could turn into drunken brawls. Another rule, of course, was that there would be no drinking. Considering that prohibition had just ended, that was probably a wise rule.

The first dance was to be held at the Rutledge house, where there were a large living room and a piano. Actually there was a piano in nearly every ranch home. Mother raised turkeys for two years and saved money to buy a piano for me. Other parents also had visions of sons and daughters astonishing the neighbors as they sat down to play. So the pianos were ordered, and trundled over the dirt roads in rickety trucks, inching down Reif Hill from Clayton or jolting endlessly down the hundred miles from Trinidad.

The piano was certainly wasted on me. I was a bright kid, even at six, and I realized at some level that music was not for me. I couldn't sing a lick. Mother had a nice voice, and Dad sang a robust baritone; my brothers and sisters could sing a tune, but not me. Mother pleaded, cajoled, and threatened, but nothing could tie me to that piano bench. I probably took more piano lessons with less accomplishment than anyone in the world.

The big night finally arrived. Laura Gay and Peggy were at my house, and we got ready in a delicious whirl of giggles, whispers, and supposings. We bathed in tin washtubs and combed out our curls. Mother had put my hair up in rags, and every other mother's daughter had had her stringy hair interfered with in some way. We harnessed ourselves, flat chests and all, into flesh-colored (pink) bras and garter belts. We pulled silk hose over our scabby knees and put on our high heels. We dabbed Mum in each abraded armpit. We sat at the dresser with a kerosene lamp at each side and put on our Tangee and light pink powder. We probably looked like a bunch of clowns, but we felt beautiful. Then we put on our long dresses and Evening in Paris and went to the dance.

One might fear that after all the anticipation and preparation the actual event might be a letdown, a disappointment in some way, but it was not. It was magic. Mrs. Rutledge had decorated the room with crepe-paper streamers, with candles on the mantelpiece. The kerosene lamps were turned low. The boys, unnaturally clean and quiet, stood against the wall by the fireplace. Mrs. Behimer took her seat on the piano bench and began to play. The boys all stood there during the whole first set while the girls looked everywhere but at the boys. The music began again, and Jiggs Collins took Betty Easley by the hand and moved out on the dance floor. Jack Rutledge asked me to dance, and John asked Laura Gay. The others stepped out. It was wonderful. Everyone acted polite and civilized, and no one fell down. We managed the more exuberant folk dances and whirled acceptably in the waltz. Then we had refreshments. The girls had brought cake or sandwiches, and the boys had contributed a small amount of money to buy the soft drinks.

I think often of those dances. I realize they surely were not as grand as my memory insists, but they were extraordinary. I think of Ada Behimer pounding on that piano by the hour, relieved occasionally by Milly Easley, who could play anything she had ever heard.

I think of the parents, in the middle of drought and the

Great Depression, struggling to give their children some sort of entertainment and a few social graces. So the dances continued every two weeks, at the Behimer house or at the Rutledges', and once at our new ranch home.

The dance club, of course, did not knock off all our rough edges, but it did smooth out some of them. The boys and girls of the Valley added a new set of words to the vocabulary they used with each other, words such as "Please" and "Thank you" and "You're welcome." This vocabulary and other small courtesies were new experiences for us all and very useful for the rest of our lives.

Chapter 7

Celebrations

The photographs I found in Arkansas have evoked a number of memories that astonish me. No photograph retrieved so many memories for me as did the picture of Cora, a singer, and a decorated Christmas tree. Once Sandy and I tried to recreate Cora's tree. We had the paper chains and the cutout paper stars. There were no electric lights and only a few glass balls. We didn't do the popcorn strings because we remembered how terribly tedious that chore was. It takes an immense amount of popcorn because it crumbles when the needle is thrust through it. Anyone stringing popcorn soon winds up with a drift of popcorn fragments around the feet. There are other strings on Cora's tree, some of which may be cranberries. I remember stringing the cranberries for the tree in our little one-room school. We thought they were beautiful, and they were, glistening in the lamplight. The photograph of Cora's tree was taken in 1917 at Star Prairie

School in South Dakota, but the tree is generic. It flourished in all the little one-room schoolhouses across the
plains and down in the breaks in the homestead years.

The first Christmas I remember was at Model, Colorado, the little town on the Colorado flats near the homestead where I was born. It was before we moved down
into the Cimarron Valley, so I must have been around
three. I also must have been a self-centered, covetous
little pig, because I remember being sure that each gift
Santa Claus brought down the aisle must certainly be for
me. However, child after child received a present, the pile
of presents was getting smaller, and I became convinced
that I had been passed over. I could stand it no longer, and
as Santa Claus passed by our aisle, where I was sitting
on Dad's lap, I exploded, screaming, "Santa Claus, you
haven't brought me anything yet." I screamed it over and
over while Mother and Dad tried to hush me and all the
people laughed. Finally I saw Mother go up to the tree,
remove a small package, and hand it to Santa. He brought
it to me, and I can still recall the feeling of relief that swept
over me. It was a little gold bracelet, and it satisfied me
completely. I know now that Mother was only anxious to
subdue my frantic yelling, but I thought then, I remember
well, that Santa would not have given me anything if
Mother had not forced him to.

I know the homestead years were poor for our family;
in fact, I do not believe there were many affluent home-
steaders. Not until I was married and poor and trying to
provide Christmas presents for three, then four, then five
little children did I realize that what were, to me, lavish
Christmases on the homestead were the results of hard
work and ingenuity. I made my girls doll furniture out of

Cora's Christmas tree, with Cora at right. (Center for Southwest
Research, General Library, University of New Mexico, 992-018)

orange crates and upholstered it with scraps of old material. I hemmed little sheets and pillowcases by hand and knotted comforters. When I had finished them, I remembered them from my childhood and realized that my mother, too, had sat up nights sawing, hammering, and sewing to make our Christmas presents. I bought the dolls, of course, and I had to buy something for my son, Kelly. One year it was a windup train ordered from Montgomery Ward, one year a red wagon.

We had glorious trees, thick piñon, with the cones still hanging like little scalloped ornaments. The children and I searched all year, up and down the canyons and mesas, for just the perfect tree. We always chose and discarded several. One that looked perfect at a distance might be lopsided. Another, we would find, branched in two, and for some reason we had to have one with a good solid trunk. The day we went for the tree was always one of great excitement. We put it carefully in the back of the old blue pickup and rattled it home. Walter built the stand, and finally it was up against the east wall of the living room.

Sandy organized the little kids for stringing the popcorn and cranberries. They dragged out the box of ornaments and finally hung the tinsel that we saved from year to year. One year I saw an advertisement for icicles that glowed in the dark. Although they cost a dollar for twelve, I ordered two dozen. We were disappointed when they came. They were molded of white plastic and did look remarkably like icicles, but they did not glow. We tried them in the little hallway. Then I thought to read the directions, which informed me that the icicles had to be exposed to strong light. For a week, every time the sun shone, the kids laid the icicles on a rock outdoors. Sure enough, when we hung them on the tree and took the lamps out of the room, if we looked hard enough we could make out a ghostly green glimmer.

Several years ago Kelly went back to the old ranch house, empty then, with the windows broken and the adobe walls washing away. He happened to remember that we stored the Christmas things up between the ceiling and the roof. He climbed up through the opening in the pantry. There was old crepe paper there, and there were tinsel ropes, sodden from leaks in the roof. Kelly did find in the mess a few of those old glow-in-the-dark icicles. He took them away with him, and now they decorate his tree in Virginia.

A teddy bear hangs at the top of Cora's tree in the picture, and a lumpy white package tied with string dangles from a branch. There are a few things under the tree, but one feels that the presents have already been given out. The bear and the present were, perhaps, for some children who could not make it to the program because of distance or weather. The items under the tree must be the extra sacks of treats. When my mother taught school and sacked the treats for her school, or when the women prepared the treats for the church tree at Kenton, there were always extras in case strangers happened by or some child had been forgotten.

Once when I took my own children to the Christmas program at the Kenton Methodist Church, I caught a glimpse of May Potter's face as she watched the treats being distributed. May was a child of fifty when we came to the Valley. She lived up in a canyon with her mother, who sometimes permitted her to walk down to our place to play with us children. We adored May. I know now that

May was retarded, but then we just thought of her as a big child who loved our games and ran through the haystacks with us. She was a big woman, overweight but strong enough to pick up a child and give it a ride on her shoulders. We screamed and yelled and pretended to spur May as she galloped around our front yard.

One time Mother forgot and didn't send May home. We looked up and saw Grandma Potter speeding down the road in her buggy. She had become worried about May and had to go catch her horse and harness him to the buggy to come see about her. May knew she was in big trouble. When we saw Grandma Potter coming, we children, of course, deserted and ran to hide, leaving May to shuffle slowly across the yard to meet her mother, who was quivering with anger in the buggy. As soon as Grandma Potter was safely gone, we came out of hiding and went into the house, where Mother had just spotted Mrs. Potter and May driving back home. Mother was so upset at having forgotten the poor creature that she made Dad crank up the Model A that evening and drive to the Potters'. Mrs. Potter had already spanked May and sent her to bed. When May was finally allowed to come back again, we all made sure she got home in time, because we did not want to lose a good playmate.

When I saw the treats under Cora's tree in that photograph, I remembered May. As Sandy and I were trying to reproduce Cora's Christmas tree I told her about May, and how anxious she was. May was watching Santa Claus with total anxiety on her face. Her eyes followed every sack of candy, nuts, and oranges he passed out. Santa must have seen it, too, for he quickly handed her the brown paper sack. I was grown then, but I recognized and sympathized with the relief that spread over May's face.

Sandy and I talked about this universal fear, the fear that somehow our names were not put in the pot and that we would be overlooked or forgotten when the good things were being given out. I said, "We all know the fear and anxiety, but only in a three-year-old child or a simple soul like May is the fear manifested."

Sandy said, "Yes, we have more control. Chris didn't cry when he didn't get a present at the school party this year. He just looked all around the Christmas tree several times after all the presents had been given out. Finally Isabell, dear, sweet Isabell, noticed his distress and whispered that Geraldine had his present and he would be getting it in a day or two. He looked as relieved as you said May did."

I was so sad for the poor little fellow. "How old is Chris?" I asked Sandy.

"Thirty-five," she replied. "He teaches Business Administration."

So I am glad there were extras under Cora's tree so that no child, young or old, would have been passed by.

I think Cora's Christmas is almost over in the photograph, and the soloist is singing the final song. She stands there, so proper, with her feet at the correct angle, holding some object in her hand, singing, I hope, "Silent Night." Cora stands smiling, almost bisected by the camera, but ready, I am sure, as soon as the soloist finishes, to step forward and thank all of them for coming and to wish them all a Merry Christmas and a Happy New Year.

Christmas was not the only valued entertainment. During the depression the ranchers of the Cimarron and their wives suddenly discovered bridge. Bridge parties flourished, and lanky cowboys like Sam Rutledge and Loren Sayre began to talk knowledgeably about finesses, honors, and rubbers. No one was crazier about bridge than Dad, and no one hated it more than Mother.

Dad put me in training to be his bridge partner. I was only ten, but shuffling, dealing, and playing cards were patterned into my bones. I was a very good bridge player, able to remember the suits and figure where the cards were out against me. I don't know how I did that, but Dad and I quite often won the prizes. Of course, he was a good player too.

During the early thirties, traveling movies came to all the little towns and communities. They came hauling their own generators for electricity and set up in local schoolhouses. I don't know how they advertised their arrival—posters, perhaps, or maybe they depended on the party telephone lines. At any rate, everyone came to see the old silent movies. At Clayton, of course, there were the newfangled talking movies, but we in the Valley didn't get in to see them very often.

Besides the traveling movies, occasionally a troupe of players came out to Kenton to perform. I remember one such group. I was visiting Betty and Milly Easley, and they lived quite close to the school. I was fourteen, Milly was thirteen, and Betty was a tall fifteen. From the Easley front porch we could see persons unloading scenery, so we arose and sauntered over to the school.

The players were rehearsing. Betty, Milly, and I eased down the hall and peered around the corner to where a tap dancer was limbering up on the stage. A young man was standing by the school piano idly plunking on the keys. He saw us, smiled, and beckoned us in. The tap dancer burst into a thunderous dance and sashayed off the stage. We three sidled closer to the young man. We were all stricken mute by our encounter with the glamour of the theatre, but Betty managed to ask him if he was a performer. He told us that he sang, but his piano player was resting. "Milly plays," I blurted.

"Good," he said. "Can you play 'When I Grow Too Old To Dream?'"

Milly nodded and slid onto the bench. She began playing and the young man sang to us. I fell in love, of course, and so did Milly and Betty.

It is a measure of the depth of the Great Depression that there were persons who were willing to drive such long distances in a caravan of rickety cars and trucks. At the very most there could not have been over thirty adults at any of these shows, with perhaps as many children. At twenty-five cents for adults and ten cents for children, the take would have been very little over ten dollars for the night.

They did come, though, and offered us the magic of the theatre for very little money. The young man who sang for us three girls and thrilled us to our bones was, as I remember, a handsome lad, dressed in a neat brown suit. I was especially taken with his thin leather gloves. He very stylishly wore one and carried the other in the gloved hand. He occasionally slapped the glove into his bare palm, a bit of stage business that made me dizzy with excitement. I was seated by Betty and Milly at the performance that night. The young singer saw us and winked at me. I know he winked at me, although Betty and Milly both claimed the salute for themselves.

Although not as much fun as the movies and a great deal harder work, another important social event was spring branding. It was an honor to be invited to help at a branding. A serious protocol governed every aspect. The date was set, and early in the morning we threw the children into the back of the pickup and rattled over to the neighbor's house. The kids were turned loose to ramble over the hills or swim in the river. The women gathered in the kitchen to begin preparing the enormous noon meal, and the men went to the corral. Sometimes the younger women went out to help with the branding.

Because each man was a specialist in some aspect of branding, usually work on the calves proceeded briskly and with few hitches. One branding, however, was different. Thirty-five years ago, I wrote a story about that branding for *The New Mexico Stockman*.

THE SHORTHANDED BRANDING

The day looked like a perfect one for branding. It was so hot that even before we built the fires to heat the irons, they were too hot to touch. It seems to be an unwritten law that it must be a record-breaker of a hot day to brand calves. I have never understood this. Why not brand in the early spring? In all fairness, most people do try to get their branding done early. They try, but somehow it is always late and hot.

Buddy Boy Layton operates a ranch in the northeast corner of New Mexico, and this day was branding day. Buddy Boy is still an old-timer when it comes to branding calves. None of these sissy little calf chutes and tables for him. None of these tight little corrals where the calves can be separated from the horribly large old long-horned

Cowboys taking a short break during branding at Buddy Boy Layton's ranch, 1956. Left to right: Dixie Layton, Howard Layton, L.G. Howard, Walter Hanners, Buddy Boy Layton, Douglas Layton. (Photo by LaVerne Hanners, Collection of LaVerne Hanners)

mammies. Oh, no, he does it the old-fashioned way: with two hundred calves and their mothers gathered loosely in a wire corral about five acres in area.

In the middle of this corral was a stack of cedar wood, several buckets, a ten-gallon cream can filled with water, and the branding pit and irons. By the time we three women got on the scene, the branding fire was blazing away and the ropers were already dragging a couple of calves to the fire. To brand in a large open corral, one needs good ropers and, especially, good horses. Buddy Boy had both.

His father-in-law, Everett Smithson, was on a white horse, and his brother, Douglas, was on a snappy little bay. Everett had his calf by the neck and Doug had heeled his. They dragged the calves up to the fire, and the ground crew went into action. One man flanked a calf and another man grabbed one hind leg. Buddy Boy had the knife. My husband, Walter Hanners, was branding, and I was doing the vaccinating. Buddy Boy's wife, Deloryse, and her sister-in-law, Dixie, were kept busy replenishing the fire and keeping tally. By the time we had finished with this calf, Howard Layton and I. G. Howard had another calf on the ground.

From then on it was a madhouse of churning dirt, bawling calves, clouds of blue smoke, and stench of burning hair. The center of the corral was clear, with the majority of the calves and cows crowding close to the fence. Now and then a cow, infuriated by the bawling of the calves, would dash out toward the center, but she always turned back. It never failed to scare me nearly to death, though, and I shamelessly got behind whoever happened to be standing close.

I was elected to run the needle because I had had a little experience and because foolishly enough I had volunteered. Vaccinating is not too hard. One merely leans over the back of the calf—while he is being held securely on the ground, of course, picks up a handful of hide, pushes in the needle, presses down the plunger, removes the needle, and leaps toward the next calf. The only thing: the hide is tough. The jabbing of the needle amounts to the expenditure of enough energy to pick up a large rock and throw it several feet. The branders are coming behind you with hot irons and you are bending over in a very insecure position.

We were branding like clockwork. The calves were being worked with great speed, when suddenly we were out two men. A calf Everett was roping broke in an unexpected direction, jerking the rope across Everett's ribs. He was in such pain that he and his wife decided he had better see a doctor. The boy they had brought went back with them, and we were short three vital hands: a roper, a flanker, and a cook.

Buddy Boy stood by the branding fire, scratching his head and looking at his wife and Dixie. "Dee," he said, "you could flank some of these calves, couldn't you? Some of the little ones, I mean."

"Flank calves?" Dee laughed. "Why, certainly, certainly. How do I do it?"

"Nothing to it. Just lean over his back, grab a front leg and his flank, boost him in the ribs with your knee, and he'll go down." Buddy Boy trotted off to work on another calf.

"Oh, certainly, certainly, certainly. Nothing to it," Dee muttered and grabbed a calf. She followed directions and the calf went down. "Come on, Dixie," she yelled. "This is fun." From then on, Dee and Dixie worked as a crew, throwing the calves with the ease of professionals. They did let the men throw the larger ones, however.

We worked and worked. The sun seemed stuck in the sky, slightly east of center. The water in the cream can was hot enough to scald a hog. We were gasping for breath. Mercifully, Buddy Boy called a halt. "Let's go in for dinner now. We've got more than half of them."

We three women looked at each other. Dinner. We had forgotten all about dinner. Our teenaged daughters were watching the little kids, but we knew better than to hope that they might have cooked dinner. "I'd run away but I'm too tired," Dee said, throwing herself on the ground. "Kill me with a rock, someone, cause I'm too far gone to live and I don't want to suffer."

We persuaded her to her feet and lurched into the kitchen. We washed the dirt from our hands and faces and started frying chicken, while the men lounged on the nice cool, shady porch and let ice-cold beer trickle down their throats. Finally dinner was ready. We fed the children and the men. Then we sat wearily down at the table, almost too tired to eat. Buddy Boy was already hovering in the door.

"Well, girls—" he started to say, but Deloryse froze him with an awful look.

"Look, my darling husband. If you want us three able-bodied women to go back out there to that dusty corral to do your branding, you are going to give us enough time to eat our dinner, and comb our hair, and put on some more lipstick."

"Yeah," Dixie chimed in. "Or maybe we might get

sick, and not be able to help you at all." I didn't say a thing. I just sat there trying to look sickly.

There really is such a thing a second wind. I had never believed it before, but as the long afternoon wore on, all were able to keep working. It began to seem vaccinating calves was a way of life, that I had always vaccinated calves, and would do so into eternity. Once when there was a short lull, I flung myself on the ground behind the cream cans and tried to look small and invisible. I got a good forty-three-second rest before I heard one of the men yelling, "Needle. Needle."

I jumped to my feet shouting, "Mush! Mush! On to Nome! The serum must go through." Crazy as a coot, of course.

Then suddenly, incredibly, it was over. I heard Buddy Boy bawl, "Well, that's all. Turn them out."

Dixie, Dee, and I immediately fell to the ground. Buddy Boy ambled over to us. "Well, girls, with a little more practice you wouldn't be bad help."

I smiled at Dee and Dixie. "Shall we?" I murmured. They smiled at me. We rose as one woman and launched ourselves at Buddy Boy. Dee and Dixie flanked him and threw him, and Buddy Boy really thought for a minute there that I was going to vaccinate him.

The burial of the dead was another occasion when the community always came together. These were sad occasions, to be sure, but in the response and gathering of neighbors, the solemn rituals, and the tender regard of the living toward the dead, funerals were celebrations of a sort.

Jiggs Collins died on August 11, 1991. I went to Kenton

with Kelly to stand with my children at the funeral of their father. The funeral was at the Kenton Methodist Church, and Jiggs's friends came from everywhere to pay tribute to this rollicking cowboy—Old Man Coyote, jokester, trickster, doting father, tender lover, calamitous husband. No one would have wished him back, ill as he was and in such torment. Jiggs's death released us to great memories, outrageous tales, and hearty laughter. It was an old-fashioned Kenton, Oklahoma, kind of funeral with pallbearers and honorary pallbearers, all childhood friends.

One goes up a short flight of stairs into the sanctuary of the church. At the right, there is a small area where the men had placed their cowboy hats. These hats were upside down, resting on their crowns, and looking particularly forlorn separated from their owners.

The Stetson hat is such an integral part of any cowboy that Jeanne brought one of Jiggs's old Stetsons from Flagstaff. She slid it under the unopened half-lid of the coffin and rested it on his knees. Sandy became upset because she had not thought to bring an Indian artifact or at least a piece of flint to put with Jiggs, so her Uncle Bob, Jiggs's youngest brother, gave her an Indian knife of chipped flint, and Sandy put it in the pocket of Jiggs's Levis. I don't know exactly why they did these things, but it seemed to comfort them, and that is good enough reason. I think Jeanne just couldn't bear to send that old cowboy off without his hat. Neither could Sandy stand for the greatest of relic hunters to be without a single piece of worked flint.

So we sat through the services and the songs. Then we followed the hearse up to the slope above Kenton.

When I think of the persons I grew up with, I think of the dance at our new house on my fourteenth birthday. All the boys and girls of my age were there, and now there are few left alive. My two brothers survive, but my sisters have been dead for many years. Buddy Boy Layton and his brother Howard are still with us. Everett Like lives on his dad's old place up Flathead Canyon, and Bud Henry and Peggy Davis are still alive and well. There may be more, but I do not know of them. Jiggs's mother, Marion Collins, still lives, alert at ninety-six, although blind, and my dear old teacher, Kathryn Quimby, is still alive, although she really left us many years ago. She left us a little at a time until finally there was nothing left but her breath and heartbeat. She taught us so much, so well, and I am ever grateful to her.

We sat beside Jiggs's open grave. The military honor guard folded the flag and gave it to Kelly, we bowed our heads for the benediction, and it was over. We went back to the church basement, where the ladies of the community served incredible food in incredible amounts. We ate and talked and laughed. Jeanne and Sandy and their husbands went back to their homes, and Kelly and I drove back to Clayton and then to Springer, Las Vegas, and on below Albuquerque.

I miss Jiggs more than I could have imagined. We were married when we were hardly more than children, and we had been divorced for forty-eight years. He was, except for his mother and my two brothers, the person I had known longest. He was the friend of my childhood and the husband of my youth. The earth has become a duller place without him.

Chapter 8

Calamities

The Valley was a long way from a doctor. It was one hundred miles up the river to Trinidad and at least forty south to Clayton. Kenton had a doctor once early in the century, but she married and retired. Boise City had a doctor during the twenties and thirties, but he had no hospital.

Not only was it a great distance to town—any town—but the roads were terrible. The road that went by the ranch called itself a national highway, but really it was little more than a wagon trail, fixed up a bit for cars.

Clayton had a nice little hospital, perhaps ten beds, run by the Sisters of Mercy and head nurse, Sister Teresina. Sister Teresina was a formidable woman, tall and thin with piercing black eyes. Most people were scared of Sister Teresina. She stood for no nonsense. If you were due an injection, down went the covers, up went the shirttail, and you were shot in record time. A wail of anguish didn't bother Sister Teresina at all.

Sister met her match just once. Raymond Sumpter was driving his father-in-law, Ike Like, into Clayton in their old, cut-down Model A truck. Something important broke on the vehicle, and Raymond couldn't control the car. It turned over and threw Mr. Like out and broke his leg. Raymond flagged down a car and got Mr. Like into the hospital with a cast on his leg and outrage in his heart.

Ike Like was probably the world's worst patient. He did not wish to be bathed by women, so one of his several sons or Raymond made the trip into town to wash him down. He didn't like the food, so one of the family brought him his meals from the Eklund Tavern. Above all, Mr. Like was not satisfied with the amount of ice he could have with his water. Every day he had a hundred pounds of ice delivered to the hospital steps. People made excuses to drive by the hospital so they could see the block of ice melting in the sun. Mr. Like's neighbors were proud of him, especially those who had been gunned down by Sister Teresina's hypodermic needle.

Broken bones were common disasters. Raymond Sumpter and Mr. Like were already nearly to Clayton when Mr. Like's leg got broken. If he had been near Kenton, it is likely that Raymond would have taken him to Mr. Eddy. W. M. Eddy ran the post office in Kenton and sold medicines, candy, a few magazines, and ice. He also practiced a frontier kind of medicine. Mr. Eddy's only training was experience, but he was skillful. He could stitch up wounds and set bones. He ordered patent medicines by the gallon. He gave us kids a penny apiece for all old medicine bottles we brought to him. These bottles he filled with various nostrums, most of which appear to have been harmless. At least he knew the principles of disinfecting, and he knew when he was out of his depth. If Mr. Eddy couldn't fix it, he sent one on to the doctor in Clayton or Trinidad.

Mr. Eddy was a godsend to the Valley, if for nothing else, for a rough sort of triage. If Mr. Eddy said to go to a doctor, people went, and if he said he could fix it, people believed.

The doctors or Mr. Eddy were for emergencies only. Mostly, people medicated themselves. It is amazing that they did so little harm. Mother was big on poultices, plasters, and castor oil. If anyone cut a foot, Mother put a bread-and-milk poultice on the wound. This poultice was supposed to "draw out the poison." I expect we survived because the air, water, and soil were clean and infections uncommon for that reason. I just can't believe that a slab of home-baked bread soaked in milk and bandaged over a cut could have any medicinal value at all. Perhaps the mustard plasters Mother slapped on our chests when we had colds were of some benefit. Those plasters stung and burned and turned our skin bright red. If nothing else, they imbued us with a desperate will to get well.

Castor oil also was a great influence on our medical behavior. If we mentioned having even the slightest pain in our stomachs, Mother cornered us to administer the most noxious cure known to the healing arts. She laid it all out on the kitchen table. First she dropped a table-spoon of castor oil into a cup of orange juice and mixed it all up. Then she put in a teaspoon of baking soda and stirred it again. When the mixture was foaming good she made us drink it. There was no escape. We had to try. Of course when the awful stuff hit the back of our throats we started to throw up, but Mother was ready for that. She beat us in the face with a wet towel until we quit retching. I don't think I took any permanent damage from Mother's castor-oil treatment, although I was forty before I ate an orange and I still don't like them very much.

Someone must have alerted Mother to the hazards of combining stomach pain and castor oil, for she quit using it.

The little Easley boy was not so fortunate. Bill Easley and his two children lived back up a canyon in the south mesas of the Valley. We were living on the Smylie place then, on our own ranch, in the summer of 1936. I looked to the west and saw a man come walking across the northwest pasture heading toward our house. In that spacious land a walking person was a sure sign of trouble, so John got in the car and drove to meet him. It was Bill Easley. John brought him in haste to the house. Bill said to Mother, "Mrs. Goodson, my boy's awful sick. He had a pain in his stomach and I gave him a big dose of Epsom salts. Could John take us to Clayton?"

John and Bill left, and it seemed only a few minutes until we saw the car heading toward Clayton. A high plume of dust rose behind the car, an indication of great speed. John came home late that night to tell us that the little boy was safe, but that his appendix had ruptured. This may have been when Mother stopped her castor-oil treatment.

There was so much danger. From early spring until late fall there was the danger of snakes. At that time rattlesnakes abounded in that country, and quite frequently someone was bitten. Wesley Labrier was building fence when a rattler struck him on the leg. Mother and we children were coming into Kenton when the Labrier car swerved around the corner heading for Clayton. The plume of dust from that car towered high into the air. One could almost estimate the severity of the emergency by the height of the dust cast by the wheels. When we saw the car coming we knew there was big trouble. Wesley recovered from the snakebite and luckily was not killed on that wild ride to town.

Jiggs Collins was struck on the finger of his right hand. The snakebite didn't bother him much, but he had an allergic reaction to the antivenom and had to stay in the hospital several days longer than usual.

A little girl out by Seneca was struck in the thigh. She and her parents were working in their garden, and the child stumbled and fell on the snake. They started for Clayton in such a frantic hurry that they threw another girl out of the back end of the pickup and broke her leg. The child who was bitten lived only four hours. The doctor at the hospital at Clayton could not save her, for the snake was a large one and its fangs had gone directly into a vein.

Our ranch was infested with snakes. Some were harmless sorts, useful for keeping down rodents. Some of the snakes were, of course, rattlesnakes. We all watched for snakes at all times on, I believe, a subconscious level and were hardly ever surprised by them. We killed the rattlers and let the others go.

There were two times when snakes did take me by surprise, and those two times remain in my memory as two of my most frightening experiences.

Once, when I was married to Walter, I was alone on the ranch with my three oldest children, Sandy, Jeanne, and Kelly. I had brought in the milk cows, and I turned to the stacks of baled hay to get some to put in the manger. I leaned down to pick up a section of hay and realized that I was looking directly into the eyes of a rattlesnake, only inches from my face.

The next thing I knew I was on top of the cowshed. I don't know if there is something about panic that clears the sight, but as I looked down I saw the snake still coiled on the bale of hay. I could see his rattles and even his fangs as he raised his head and hissed.

I climbed down from the barn and told Sandy to go get the little single-shot rifle. I knew I had only one bullet; I had seen it tumbling about in a small drawer full of junk. I told Sandy where the bullet was, and she went to the house and came back immediately with the gun and the bullet. I shot the snake's head off.

That day panic drove me in a mad flight away from a snake, but one time panic took me in a wild run toward a snake. Mother and I were behind the house getting the garden ready for spading. It was a bright, warm day, so I had brought Jeanne out and put her on a blanket in the sunshine. She was just old enough to sit alone. Mother thrust a pitchfork under a pile of dried weeds and lifted them up. A small rattler flashed out from under the weeds, crossed the blanket, and ran up on my baby's lap. The snake attempted to crawl around Jeanne's neck, but Jeanne turned her head trying to look at the strange animal. The snake then wavered to the other side of Jeanne's face.

Again panic seemed to clear my vision and I could see my baby and the rattlesnake doing a little dance, Jeanne's head moving from side to side and the snake weaving back and forth. I crossed the garden in three bounds, reached down—still in full stride, and grabbed the snake right behind his head. Then I threw him. I threw that snake so hard that he sailed, turning and twisting, over Mother's head and clear out of the garden. Mother's back was turned and she had no idea what was happening. She saw a snake writhing in the air as it passed over her head, and she stood staring at the unbelievable sight.

I hear people say, "Don't panic," and that's dumb. Both those incidents with a snake could have been fatal, for a snakebite in the face will almost always kill. Panic guided me to do the correct thing both times. Climbing a shed to get away from a snake was probably excessive, but flight was certainly the way to preserve myself. Panic served me well when I saw the snake on Jeanne and helped me do everything exactly right.

Sometimes, of course, panic is not all that useful. The story is told in the Valley of a rancher who was snakebit when he dismounted to open a gate. He ran right past his horse a quarter mile to his house. The story was told about two or three different ranchers, all of whom denied it when questioned, so perhaps it didn't happen.

Neither have I been able to discover a source for the story of the abandoned baby. It seems that a rancher's wife gave birth in the car on the way to Clayton. The father wrapped the baby in a blanket and laid it down at the side of the road while he tended to his wife. Then he jumped in the car and went hell-bent to the hospital. When he got there Sister Teresina quite naturally said, "Where is the baby?" The aghast father jumped back in the car and drove hell-bent back down the highway, where his first child was screaming his lungs out at the side of the road.

Whether apocryphal or not, both stories illustrate the need for haste (sometimes overdone) during any emergency. One such emergency nearly took the life of my brother John's oldest child, Johna Gale, a little girl of about three.

John and his wife, Norene, were living on the ranch. It was during the war, and Felix was already a prisoner. Felix's old black dog, called Mustard for some reason, was old when Felix went to the army. Before he left, Felix asked us to take care of his dog. We all felt Mustard was a sacred trust, even though he was quite old and cross. He snapped at the little Capansky boy, and Mother tried to get the boy's father to put Mustard down, but Glenn refused, saying he just wasn't going to kill that old dog, Felix being in a prison camp and all.

One night, John, Norene, and Johna Gale were sitting outside in the hammock when Gale decided to go into the house. Mustard was sleeping in the doorway. Gale stepped on Mustard's foot, and the dog came up from a sound sleep and snapped at Gale's face. A tooth went directly through the artery in Gale's temple. She collapsed in a pool of blood on the kitchen floor. A neighbor woman who was visiting picked Gale up, screamed, and handed the child to Norene, who had come running through the door. Norene screamed and handed Gale to John, who saw the terrible spray of blood and groaned, "Her throat's cut." John gave Gale to Mother and ran to get the ax to kill the dog. He came to himself when he saw the car. He jumped in and brought it around to the gate.

There was so much blood Mother could not tell where it was coming from, but she kept pressing on Gale's face and neck until, suddenly, the great gush of blood stopped. Mother could not be sure which finger was closing off the artery, so she held her hand rigidly in place as she carried Gale to the car. On the way to Clayton, Mother did not move her hand.

Mother had on one shoe, and Norene was barefoot. They all were covered with blood. John looked at the gas gauge and realized he didn't have enough gas to get to Clayton, so he stopped at Moses Store. Isaac Martinez, the owner, had already gone to bed, and the store was dark. John pounded on Isaac's window. "Isaac, this is John Goodson. I've got to have some gas."

"Now, John, I'm in bed, and I was asleep. You go on. You've probably got enough gas. I'm not getting up."

John said, "Isaac—now. My baby's hurt bad. Now."

The urgency in John's voice alerted Isaac, and he came to the gas pump in his bare feet. He cast a horrified look into the car, where Mother and Norene and Gale sat covered with blood.

"Oh, my God, Mrs. Goodson, I'm so sorry. I'm so sorry. I didn't know." When John dug into his pocket to pay for the gas, Isaac waved him on. "John, go. And hurry."

They got to the hospital, and Sister offered to take Gale from Mother, but Mother held on to Gale, not willing to risk moving her hand. When the doctor got there, Mother put Gale on the operating table and finally took her hand from Gale's face.

The blood had clotted and had stopped flowing. The doctor couldn't see the wound. Of course he could see all the blood, but he couldn't see where it had come from. "Well," he said, "this doesn't seem so bad." He tugged at a lock of hair matted to Gale's head and the blood blasted into his face. Sister Teresina was there, thank God, and stopped the blood while the doctor cleaned his glasses.

Mother, of course, was a giant in any emergency, but that little three-year-old girl was remarkable also. She realized somehow that her survival depended on her remaining absolutely quiet. She was frightened and in pain, but she did not cry or move all that long way to Clayton.

When Walter and I were on the ranch, Nell tripped and cut an artery high on the side of her forehead. I had never seen arterial bleeding before, but I recognized it immediately although there was only a light spray. Walter also recognized it, and ran to the medicine cabinet. He came back with a can of powder. He sifted it on Nell's head and the bleeding stopped immediately. Wherever the powder touched blood it turned black. Walter had sprinkled Nell's head with a powder used to stop the bleeding when cattle were dehorned. It was wonderfully effective on Nell, but it would not have worked on the massive flow of blood from Gale's head.

I was so afraid I would cause Nell's wound to open that I did not wash her hair for two weeks. She went to church twice with half of one side of her head blackened with the powder. I washed her a bit around the neck and ears, but I might have left her head unwashed for a year if Walter had not convinced me that Nell's head was healed.

Once when we were on the Roberts Ranch, Mother heard a pounding on the door. When she opened the door she saw Charles Robinson standing there. His face was white and covered with beads of sweat. Charles held up his hand. "Mrs. Goodson, I just shot myself in the hand." Then he pitched forward in a faint. Mother caught him and eased him to the floor. Then she ran to the phone. The parents of the young man were on their way to Clayton with Dad and had left only a short time before.

Mother called Moses Store and told them to run out and flag down Felix Goodson and send him back, that the Robinson boy had shot himself in the hand. Mother wrapped the boy's hand in a towel and propped his feet up on a chair. I brought her a wet washcloth to wipe Charles's face, then went to look for Dad. Sooner than seemed possible, I saw the Model A come through the gap and hurtle down the road to the house.

John was with Dad that day. I called John not long ago to ask him about this incident. He said the man at Moses Store had misunderstood Mother and thought she said the boy was shot in the head. John said it was really a wild ride, bucking and bouncing at high speed over the ruts and rocks of that old dirt road.

My own ordeal and long ride to Clayton happened in 1943. I was six months pregnant with Kelly. Jiggs and I were living on Carrizozo Creek, miles away from the nearest neighbors.

I woke in the middle of the night with a terrible pain in my stomach. I was nauseated and felt sick enough to die. I woke Jiggs and told him he would have to go for help. He asked me if I could possibly hang on until daylight. I knew why Jiggs asked. He had to go across a pasture to the north of us, a pasture that was infested with prairie dogs. The night was very dark, and the prairie-dog holes were a great danger to horses. It would not help me if Jiggs was thrown, or if his horse broke a leg. He could have gone by the road, but this would have added miles to his journey.

Jiggs built a fire, as it was December and cold in the house. Then he went out to saddle his horse and begin a seven-mile ride through the pitch dark to Roy Belding's house. When he was gone I knelt in my big rocker and held on to the back. That position seemed to give me some relief from the intense pain. I don't think I was very coherent, but I kept trying to plan what to do if Jiggs did not get back. I decided that if he was not there by sunup I would wake Sandy and tell her to walk toward Kenton. It was only two miles to the highway. I reasoned that if she could reach the highway someone would pick her up and come to our rescue. I think she could have done it, although she was just barely four years old. Once I had a plan to save the lives of my two children, I gave myself over to the pain and illness and just waited. I may have been unconscious some of the time, or at least in a stupor, for it didn't seem long until I heard Mother's voice. She and John and Roy and Jiggs came in. Roy had driven Jiggs to Mother's to get her to come for the children. Mother and John came with her car so John and Jiggs could take me to Clayton. Roy drove Mother and the little girls back to the ranch in his truck.

I don't remember the trip to Clayton, but I remember arriving at the hospital at about three in the morning. I was very thin, and I looked ready to deliver the baby even though I was just six months pregnant. Perhaps there is some excuse for the nightmare that followed. There was a middle-aged person working on the floor. I remember thinking at the time that she was the janitor. At any rate she was not a Sister, nor was she a nurse. Jiggs and John helped me to the room, and the woman put me to bed. Then she called my doctor and told him I was in the hospital having pains. He told her to start timing my pains, and she even brought a clock to my bedside and told me to ring the bell when they got five minutes apart. John and Jiggs left, thinking I was in good hands. They went to the Eklund Hotel and got a room. I pushed the bell and the woman came back in. I said to her, "Look, I'm terribly sick. Could you please call one of the Sisters."

"I can't do that unless it's an emergency," she said, and she left. I waited a little, then rang the bell again. When the woman came back I resorted to profanity, begging and pleading and swearing. This time she told me I could go to hell for talking like that and she took away my bell.

Then I believed that I would die, and of course by this time I didn't care. I was glad Sandy and Jeanne were safe. I didn't have the strength to scream, and I couldn't get out of bed, so I just endured. I don't think I was asleep, but again in a sort of coma. I came up out of that stupor as it was getting daylight. Sister Teresina was leaning over my bed. "Sister," I whispered, "they're going to let me die." She put a hand on my face and left, her starched white habit swirling. In no time my doctor was there, and John and Jiggs were there, and Sister was there with that blessed hypo in her hand. That hypo was taking effect as I heard the doctor say, "You have acute appendicitis, and I'm sending you to Raton." He also warned me that I would probably lose the baby.

Sister Teresina packed me in ice, and we began the hundred-mile trip to Raton to Miners' Hospital. They were waiting for me when I got there, but all I remember were the shears they used to cut off my clothes. Kelly and I survived the surgery, and I carried him to term. But I often thought (and hoped) that the night attendant and my doctor barely survived Sister Teresina.

Chapter 9

Drought and the Great Depression

The drought came to the Valley slowly. Nineteen thirty was a fairly good year, and the next year was not too bad. There was very little rain in 1932 and almost none for the next five years. A little water still flowed down the Cimarron, and there were the floods.

As the drought worsened the vegetation dried up and blew away, and the ground turned into hardpan. Any rain that fell upriver immediately headed downhill, scouring off the topsoil and flooding the Cimarron. While the water from the dams on the Cimarron was carefully apportioned, floodwater was free.

The telephone would ring five rings, the signal for everyone on the line to pick up the receiver, and a rancher from upriver would announce that they had had a shower and that a small head of water was coming down the

Cimarron. Day or night, Dad rousted out the hands, put on his irrigation boots, and grabbed a shovel. They all headed for the sluices and head gates to send the water out over the alfalfa fields. The floods saved the hay, but nothing could save the grazing lands.

Raising cattle for beef was predicated on the animals' being able to graze. Hay was too expensive, and there wasn't enough of it to feed range cattle. The hay went to dairy cattle, horses, and young heifers that were calving. Men came from Kansas, Nebraska, and even farther north to try to buy enough hay to save their dairy herds.

The weather was erratic the first year or two of the drought. Even though we were dried out in the Valley, still to the north of us there was some rain, and some grass grew. Dad and Shorty Quimby leased grassland on Barella Mesa west of Trinidad, and they began the trail drive northwest. Seven cowboys, a cook, the trail boss, and two boys started twelve hundred head of cattle up the Valley of the Cimarron.

The trail boss was Bob Wagner, and R. B. Eddy was the cook. John could remember the names of three of the cowboys—Doodle Freeman, Sam Rutledge, and Albert Cochran. John went along on Peewee as a working hand. He was twelve, and as useful as a full-grown man. They were grazing the cattle along and did not expect to make good time. Felix had begged to be allowed to go, so Mother let him get in the chuck wagon with R. B. even though Felix was not quite eight years old. She also stuck an old black umbrella in his hands as a protection from the sun. The chuck wagon always went ahead to pick out a good campsite and to have the meal ready when the men got there.

The second day out, five of the cowboys came riding up to the chuck wagon for their noon meal. Felix suddenly leaned out from the wagon and snapped his umbrella open right in the horses' faces. The horses spooked. They reared and bucked, and one of them threw his rider. The rest of the cowboys finally got their horses calmed down. When the men dismounted they grimly advanced on Felix, who by this time had sought safety behind R. B. R. B. did not allow them to kill Felix, as R. B. had promised Mother he would take care of him.

Once Dad brought Mother, the two little girls, and me up the river to the noon camp. We ate lunch with the cowboys. There were fried steaks, and gravy and fried potatoes and pinto beans, canned tomatoes and canned peaches, and those wonderful biscuits baked in the dutch oven. The huge enameled coffeepot hung over the campfire, and R. B. stabbed open a can of condensed milk so the men could have cream with their coffee.

It was on this trail drive that John had had his strange accident with the rope around his neck. John was sitting in the chuck wagon when Dad arrived from home to check on the progress of the drive. John was dipping an old rag in cold water and patting the severe rope burns on his neck. Dad threw John in the car and drove like fury to the doctor in Trinidad. The doctor medicated the rope burns and gave John a whopping shot of morphine. John went to sleep in the back seat of the car and Dad drove to the bank.

He went into Mr. Jeffries's office, and when Mr. Jeffries saw Dad's stricken face he jumped to his feet and said, "My God, Felix, what's wrong?" Dad sat down and threw his head down on Mr. Jeffries's desk and went into hysterical weeping. Dad was sobbing so hard that Mr. Jeffries couldn't understand what was wrong. Dad finally managed to gasp out something about John, and Mr. Jeffries, of course, thought Dad had lost his oldest son. That situation was resolved by John's tottering through the door, bandaged and woozy but certainly alive.

Dad was foolish about his children and went demented when anything happened to one of us. John broke his arm once, and Dad brought him to the house. Dad came in alone, probably with the idea of breaking the news gently to Mother. He came into the room slowly, looking all around. Mother quite naturally said, "What are you looking for?"

Dad said, "I'm looking for a place to lay little John," and burst into sobs. Mother rushed past Dad and into the yard to see a cowboy helping John out of the car. Peewee had managed to unseat John somehow, and John broke his arm when he fell. Mother was furious that Dad had frightened her.

There was another time that Dad really alarmed Mother. He was sitting in his big rocking chair when suddenly he put his hands up to his face and began weeping. Mother envisioned all sorts of calamities and jumped up saying, "What is it, Felix? What? What?"

Dad took his hands away from his face and, still sobbing, said, "Oh, Stel, I just got to thinking. We have five kids, and the odds are we'll lose one of them before we die, and I just don't think I can stand it." Dad was so big and so aggressively masculine that it didn't bother him a bit to cry. Mother never cried at all. Not ever. I saw her almost cry once. I had been into Kenton, and in the mail was the telegram from the War Department saying that my brother Felix's name was on the Red Cross list of prisoners of war. Mother put her head down and gave two dry sobs. Then she put that worry aside. She had complete faith in Felix's ability to survive, and nothing infuriated her more than for some sadistic numskull to say (and they did it a lot), "Oh, Mrs. Goodson, I'm so sorry. I'd just rather a son of mine be dead than a prisoner of the Japanese." Of course when Felix came home three years later everyone said, "I knew all along he was going to make it."

Some of the photographs I picked up in the flea market in Benton, Arkansas, were of farms and crops and farm machinery. There are photos of persons standing in a field with their arms stretched out over chest-high wheat. And there are photographs of incredibly abundant harvests. It makes a person cringe to see those photographs. We know what is coming, and we know how soon it will be there: the Great Drought and Dust Bowl.

At the turn of the century settlers rushed to the prairies and river bottoms of the midsection of America. They came in hordes after World War I. They came in immigrant trains and in Model Ts and even with wagons and teams. The settlers scattered out on their sections, half-sections, and quarter-sections and put up tar-paper shacks or shoveled out dugouts. The Indians were on reservations and the land was free, so the settlers set their plows and ripped open the prairie. The soil had lain fallow since the beginning of the universe, and the crops from that soil were phenomenal. Kansas, Nebraska, the Dakotas, Oklahoma, eastern Colorado, northern New Mexico, and the Panhandle of Texas grew green and lush with wheat, corn, beets, maize, and other food and feed

Threshing wheat at Willowbar, Oklahoma, ca. 1921. (Center for Southwest Research, General Library, University of New Mexico, 992-018)

crops. Then the rains stopped. The soil, no longer bound by the tough roots of the buffalo grass, dried, caked, and then powdered. A dust as fine as flour lifted up from the earth and mixed with the air and began to move with the faintest current of wind.

The worst dust storms came from the north and northwest, although they could come with wind from any direction. They came silently and were absolutely terrifying. The storms loomed up over the Black Mesa and dropped down from the cap rocks and into the canyons like moving water.

The very worst storm was that of April 14, 1935. It hit in the afternoon at about 5:15. I saw it for just a second. Mother and I were the only persons at the ranch. John was at the Rutledge house, Felix was at the Cochran place, and Dad, Fred, Barbara, and Virginia had gone in to Kenton. Mother and I were sitting in the south bedroom sorting and tearing cloth into strips for a rag rug. The sun was bright in the front yard, and I had let our beautiful Persian kitten, Smoky, out to explore.

Suddenly Mother got up and went outside and around the corner of the house. I heard her scream, "It's a cyclone." I ran out and stood looking up in terror at the golden brown wall of dust that was advancing silently toward us. It was nearly on us, turning and twisting and boiling. It looked like a great towering beast, purposeful and predatory.

Mother and I fled to the house, and I was already in the door when I remembered Smoky. I darted back into the yard, scooped up the cat, and made it back inside just before total darkness closed down. We sat on the floor at the side of the bed. The dust got thicker and thicker in the

Dust storm approaching Clayton, New Mexico. (Photo by Al Carter, Collection of LaVerne Hanners)

room, and Mother pulled a sheet over our heads to filter the dust out of the air we were breathing.

I don't know how long it lasted, perhaps two hours. Mother finally got out from under the sheet and felt her way into the kitchen and lit a lamp. There was still so much dust in the air that the lamp was just a dim glow in the room. There was dust at least an inch thick on the table, and the floor was silted over.

Dad, the girls, and Fred came home through a twilight that looked like an overexposed negative. The sun was down, and the dust that had been tawny in the sunlight had turned to shades of gray and to black in the dusk. We saw Dad's car come into the yard, the headlights barely visible through the dust that still remained in the air. Dad had started for home as soon as he could see. Virginia and Barbara were only eight and six, and they were scared to death. Dad and Fred tied handkerchiefs over the girls' mouths and noses and frightened them even more.

The four of them looked like ghosts looming through the grey air as they ran for the house. We all gathered in the kitchen, stunned at the enormity of the storm and the dust that covered everything.

Finally Mother picked up a dish towel and began to push the dust off the stove and table. Dad got a scoop shovel and with it and a broom scooped the dirt off the floor to throw out the door. Fred brought in wood and built a fire. Virginia, Barbara, and I went to the beds to take the bedding outside and shake it.

Mother must have cooked something for us; I cannot imagine what. The milk and butter were ruined. Any food already cooked, no matter how well covered, had dust in it. The only dustproof containers I can think of were Mother's cans of food, and maybe the cans that held flour and lard.

Tears from dust-irritated eyes had run down our cheeks, leaving little channels in the grime on our faces. Mother washed Barbara's face, then directed Virginia and me to the washbasin. I saw myself in the mirror that hung over the sink. My hair was dun colored, and my nostrils were black pits rimmed with mud.

The passage of a giant dust storm generated enormous amounts of static electricity. The electricity caused the dust to cling to one's body and hair. Ranchers soon learned to replace the metal cutoffs on a windmill with wooden ones. These cutoff levers were attached by a thin cable to the windmill gears and made an ideal conductor for electricity. Anyone foolish enough to grasp a metal cutoff during a dust storm could be knocked off his feet.

The Emorys were living at the Cochran place when Felix was marooned there by the storm. Felix remembered seeing Mr. Emory take a flashlight bulb out to the windmill after the storm had let up a little. Mr. Emory had attached two wires to the bulb somehow. Felix was astonished to see the bulb light up and glow brightly. I don't know what Mr. Emory hoped to prove, but I am still impressed that one person tried to make a scientific measurement of some aspect of the disaster that was falling out of the sky.

People had all sorts of theories to account for the drought and the dust storms. One favorite theory was that we were being punished for our sins. Another theory held that the big guns firing in the Japan-China skirmishes and in the Ethiopian-Italian conflict were causing all the strange weather. Of course, when the Great Dust Storm flowed over the land many people were convinced it was the end of the world.

The April 1935 storm was the biggest and one of the last of the dusters. The storms kept coming, but they did not last so long, nor were they so black and terrifying. It was also the last storm we would go through on the Roberts Ranch. We moved to our new home in June of that year, 1935.

During the early thirties, the drought claimed the full attention of the families in the Valley. The Great Depression that was plaguing the rest of the world seemed remote and of secondary importance to the struggle to keep a herd of cattle alive.

Dad sold all the cattle he could find buyers for, but there were few buyers. He shipped cattle to Chicago, but an animal had to be in good shape to make that grueling train ride, and not many of ours were. Then the government stepped in. During the early thirties, the federal government under the Agricultural Adjustment Act instituted a program of elimination. Farmers were paid to plow under crops and to destroy livestock. The program allowed Felix Goodson to sell his breeding herd to the government for ten dollars a head. Then the government paid men to shoot the cows. The cowboys took the tractor out and jerked the hides off the carcasses. Dad got fifty cents a hide.

I have since tried to explain this program to people who were outraged at the killing of cattle, just to let them lie and rot in the pasture. "Surely," some of them argued, "those cows could have been shipped to the cities and butchered and the meat given to people who were starving."

Mose and George with crops on the flats, Willowbar, Oklahoma, 1923. (Center for Southwest Research, General Library, University of New Mexico, 992-018)

It is hard to explain that the cattle were skin and bones, that there was no meat at all on those bones, and that the cattle themselves were dying. Cowboys rode the range to locate cattle that were in the worst condition, and the government men got in the pickup and raced to a dying animal to shoot it before it died. The Feds paid nothing for an animal that was already dead when the men got there. I don't know how many of Dad's cows were shot but at least a hundred were, because I remember seeing that many hides drying for shipping.

Another plague attacked the Valley along with the dust storms. Swarms of grasshoppers dropped into the Valley in such numbers that the air was iridescent with the sunlight on their wings. The grasshoppers hit the irrigated alfalfa fields with biblical devastation. Dad and the hands worked frantically trying to save the hay. They put out wheat bran mixed with poison and molasses, and grasshoppers died by the millions, but still they continued to come, swarm after swarm. The men cut metal barrels in half and welded them together. They attached the resulting troughs to the fronts of tractors. They put water and kerosene in the barrels and drove the tractors back and forth across the alfalfa fields. The barrels filled with grasshoppers, and the men dumped them out in rows at the edges of the fields. There were mountains of dead grasshoppers, and Mother had to pen her turkeys to keep them from eating the oil-tainted carcasses. The poisoning and the hopper-dozers killed tons of grasshoppers and perhaps alleviated the problem to some extent, but actually all that work did little good. They could have killed three-fourths of the grasshoppers and made very little difference. The grasshoppers were all-devouring.

They ate the leaves from trees and the bark from fence posts. They ate clothes on the line and Mother's garden. The hoppers stripped the garden in one day. Nothing stopped them until the killing frost.

The depression intruded into our lives with people, people walking down the road, hungry, lost, and without any hope at all. It seems impossible that anyone could have chosen to walk the two roads that led toward the Valley, but they came walking out of Boise City on National Highway 64. This highway ran past our ranch. The highway was only an unsurfaced dirt road and there was nothing on it, no filling stations, few houses, no water, no shelter until the road went through Kenton. From Clayton it was the same. There was a little store and post office at Moses, but between there and our ranch there was nothing on the road but a windmill.

That windmill was a godsend to travelers. Dad picked up a woman and a little boy there and brought them to the ranch. The woman had no idea where she was, and she had no destination. Even we children realized that the woman was mentally ill. Mother tried to talk to her, but the woman babbled incessantly, making little or no sense. The little boy was quiet and well behaved, but he would not leave his mother's side to come play with us.

Now in 1992, sixty years from that time, I see the pictures of the homeless on television. Of course their plight is pitiful, but to me the Great Depression is symbolized by that one homeless woman. The homeless in the cities seem almost cozy compared to that poor person wandering in the middle of a great wilderness with a small child and night coming on. There were no resources available to her, no Aid to Dependent Children, no general welfare, no food stamps, just nothing but the charity of strangers.

Mother made her and the boy a pallet on the floor. The next day Mother gave the woman a change of clothes and provided the child with some of my brothers' clothes. Dad then drove her to Trinidad and dropped her off. He gave her five dollars, and she walked off down the road heading north toward Denver.

The railroads finally gave up trying to keep men from hopping freight trains. The railroads gave them free passage, and every train through Clayton, no matter which direction it was headed, was loaded down. Men filled the empty boxcars and rode on top of the full ones. I worried then and I still worry about how all those men survived. There were a few soup kitchens in the cities, but nothing like the shelters that are available today. The men must have had little caches of food in their bedrolls. The hobo jungles along the railroads could not have helped the vast number of men who were riding the rails.

The woman and little boy were the most lost and destitute, but families came by in their old broken-down cars, heading west. The greatest number of wanderers were single men. Mother kept a tin plate, a knife and fork, and a tin cup on a bench at the kitchen door. She filled these utensils with food for the men who came several times a week walking down the road. Sometimes Dad gave the men a few days' work if he had anything at all they could do, but mostly he gave them a ride on up the Valley.

When Franklin Roosevelt was inaugurated on March 4, 1933, Dad loaded us all in the car and took us to Kenton to hear his inauguration address. We stood crowded together in Mr. Eddy's Drugs and Sundries, and listened to that cadenced voice telling us that we had nothing to fear but fear itself, and it was so. I was only eleven, but a wave of relief swept through me, and I truly felt I could leave the management of the world to Dad and Franklin Roosevelt.

With Franklin Roosevelt came the relief programs, and the men who swarmed over the land in 1930, '31, and '32 got jobs working for a survival wage—but a wage. The Civil Works Administration, later to be the Works Progress Administration, saved the lives of whole families. The young single men went to the Civilian Conservation Corps camps for a wage of thirty dollars a month. Twenty-five dollars of that monthly salary went back home to the families, salvation for the parents and younger brothers and sisters. The CCC built roads through wilderness areas, repaired dams, and cleared underbrush.

The WPA built roads, sidewalks, bridges, and public buildings. Artists painted murals in those buildings, and writers wrote those marvelous state guidebooks that are invaluable reference books even yet.

Dad was a county commissioner then, and he was determined that the Valley should have a new school. The school boards consolidated New Mexico, Wagner, and Valley schools, and Dad lobbied in Santa Fe and pulled every string he knew of, and he got the school. It was to be a wonderful school with girls' and boys' restrooms with running water and flush toilets. There would be a kitchen for hot lunches, and two classrooms, and an auditorium that could be converted to another classroom in case it was ever needed. It was built by the WPA and was finished in August of 1936. The school board named the school after Dad. They called it the Felix E. Goodson Memorial School.

Chapter 10

Taking Leave

In the stack of photographs I found in Arkansas, there is one of Cora and Bob. It was taken in 1933 "on their way to Iowa and Missouri from the claim." They were escaping. I remember that year and all the years of the thirties. Cora was escaping from a blown-out claim, from crops turned under, and from cattle starved to death. There was nothing left in the Panhandle in the thirties. Maybe Cora escaped the worst of the Great Drought. The very bad years were 1934 and 1935.

My father did not escape. He watched his range dry up and his cattle die. He tried everything. He trailed his cattle to grass, but the grass ran out. He bought hay, but there was too little of it. The dust storms continued to drop over the Black Mesa and cattle continued to die.

Dad and Mother were not really pressed for money. The family income was a princely sum for that time. Dad's salary was one hundred a month for managing the

Cora and Bob "on our way to Iowa and Missouri from the claim," ca. 1935. (Center for Southwest Research, General Library, University of New Mexico, 992-018)

Roberts Ranch, and another hundred as county commissioner. Mother made eighty a month teaching school.
That income didn't really matter. No amount of money
could make it rain or save the dying cattle.

All the money that Mother had and a great deal of
Dad's money had gone to our new house. We moved in in
the spring of 1935. The house had been building for over a
year. First the men tore down the ruins of the old Smylie
house up by the cottonwood springs. That house was
made of eighteen-inch-square adobes, four inches thick.
They saved the adobes and some of the lumber and the
doors. The lumber had been freighted in from Trinidad by
teams and wagons. The old Smylie house itself was built
with square nails. The adobes and lumber were moved to
the new site, where there was a well and a little stone
claim shack. I think Dad chose that site because of the
well and building, but it was a mistake. The new house
was built on a slope where shale was close to the surface.
There was very little topsoil, and Mother broke her heart
trying to make a garden on that barren slope.

The new house was a luxury. The living room, kitch-
en, and pantry were on the north side, and three bedrooms and a bath were on the south. I had a bedroom all
my own, with new furniture: a dresser, a four-poster bed,
and a cedar chest. Virginia and Barbara had the middle
bedroom, and Mother and Dad, of course, had the other.
John and Felix and one cowboy were out in the little stone
house. Fred Claflin did not come with us to the new
house, but retired to go back to Colorado. Our new home
was a cattle ranch only. We had no irrigation or farmland,
so we did not need all the hands there were on the
Roberts Ranch.

The new house had beautiful hardwood floors and white painted walls. Mother had bought all new furniture for the living room: a couch and chair, a dining table with chairs, and a wonderful grey carpet with flowers and vines twining around the edges. Above all, there was plumbing—a shiny white bathtub and a flush toilet.

We all loved that house. Even yet, my children and I make pilgrimages back to it. Once when we went we found the house in sad repair. The southwest corner was almost washed away, the windows were broken, and the house was full of nesting swallows. My oldest girl, Sandy, whose fine poems are published under the name Bonnie Sanford Page, was so touched by the deterioration of our old home that she wrote the following poem and has consented for me to include it here.

Two-point Perspective
By Bonnie Sanford Page

It would be hard to understand a sky
that falls all blue
to the hard-line dark of Black Mesa.
Clouds do lie along the rim rock
like soft-edge smears in white,
and evening dust leaves light there,
gold and green.
Red dirt changes in late sun,
is earth blood,
a sepia stain moving in shadow
toward the house.
The house,
brown adobe from hills torn down,

Goodson ranch house with Black Mesa in the background, ca. 1937. (Photo by LaVerne Hanners, Collection of LaVerne Hanners)

is losing clarity at the corners,
foreshortened by time.
It would be hard to understand stepping
through that doorway
into grey wings flying through
your childhood rooms,
and hard to watch the picture slide,
collide,
explode,
completely off the canvas.

The house stood vacant for a long time. We sold the ranch

to the Quimbys, and they had no need for the extra dwelling. Now, I understand, the house has been repaired and is used for a hunting lodge. I am glad of that. There are too many ruins scattered up and down the Valley.

No one loved the ranch and that house better than Dad did. He and Mother owned the claim in Colorado, of course, but that ranch up in the south mesas, and that big house, were a measure of success to Dad. I am glad he got to enjoy it for nearly a year.

Dad had been to Clayton on Saturday. He had not felt well that morning, and Mother tried to get him to stay home, but he would go. He came home shortly after dark. I remember him standing beside the dining-room table. He took bottles and packages of patent medicines out of his pockets and put them on the corner of the table. "Stella," he said, "I'm sick."

Mother put him to bed and gave him medicines, but by morning it was obvious that Dad was very sick. He had a high fever and was babbling in delirium. Mother called Shorty and George Wiggins, and they came to take Dad to the doctor. Mother got him dressed. Shorty and George arranged pillows and a quilt in the back seat of George's car and helped Dad in. I went out to the car with a brush in my hand and brushed Dad's hair. Then they went hurrying down the road, the dust pluming high behind the car.

George came back after Mother that night, and she and Sister Teresina and the doctors began the short and futile battle to save Felix Goodson's life. He lived for five days, but his heart, damaged with rheumatic fever, could not stand the strain of the pneumonia. Dad died early Friday morning, April 17, 1936.

Dad's car was at the ranch, and John and Felix and I

started off to school. The two little girls were staying at Mrs. Quimby's. Mrs. Quimby and Edna Gillespie caught up with us on the highway and signaled for us to pull over. When I saw those two women come toward our car and saw their stricken faces, I went to ground like a cornered animal. I shrank into the back seat, and when Mrs. Quimby reached for me I kicked and clawed at her. I could hear screaming and only dimly realized that those sounds were coming from my mouth. The boys sat stunned in the front seat. Mrs. Quimby and Edna Gillespie finally got me out of the back seat and into Mrs. Quimby's car. They took me to her house, where we picked up Barbara and Virginia. Then we went home.

I was sustained all the way home by the fact that Mother would be there and that somehow she could make everything right. When we came in the door Mother was standing in the kitchen, and when I saw the devastation in her face I realized that there was no help anywhere.

Dr. Wilson was there, and he gave Mother a shot—morphine I suppose—and the ladies took Mother into the bedroom and put her to bed. She hadn't slept soundly for five days, and she did go to sleep. Then Dad's youngest sister, Aunt Mary, arrived. His younger brother, Claude, lived in Folsom, and he had been with Mother in Clayton. Mother's brother, Sam, came from Oklahoma on the train. When he got there, I went in and woke her up. "Mother, Uncle Sam's here."

Mother came up out of a drugged sleep. "Sam? My brother Sam?" She seemed surprised that he was there. Uncle Paul and Uncle Bill came with Aunt Mary, but Dad's mother did not come. I don't know why Grandma Goodson or Granny Martin, Mother's mother, were not there, but they were both elderly women, and perhaps the trip would have been too much for them. I think we were all astonished at the people who came over the dirt roads, such long distances, to be with Felix Goodson's family. Ted Hanna came from Amarillo. Mr. Jeffries was there from Trinidad.

I have no idea where all these people stayed. Some, perhaps, stayed in the little hotel in Kenton. Mrs. Quimby, no doubt, put up several. There is so much I cannot remember about that desolate time. One thing I do remember, because my reaction and the reactions of my brothers were so immediate and so pronounced. They asked us if we wanted Dad's body brought back to the ranch.

I don't know why, but none of the three of us could bear the idea. We were unanimous in our horrified refusal. On Sunday the little Methodist Church in Kenton and the churchyard were crowded. The air was hot and heavy with the scent of carnations. The family sat in a small anteroom. The sermon droned on, and the choir sang, "The Old Rugged Cross." Then there was the trip behind the hearse up to the cemetery, where finally it was over.

The uncles and Aunt Mary went away. The visitors returned to their homes, and there came a day when Mother and the five of us were completely alone.

We were facing such a calamity that none of us ever shed a tear. Tears and weeping were for such things as a cut finger or a disappointment at a dance. The death of our giant, laughing, incredible father was a catastrophe of such magnitude that we hardly had a way to respond. I remember us following Mother from room to room in a little pack of five. I remember Mother trying to deal with a feeling of guilt that she hadn't made Dad's days in the hospital more comfortable. She said over and over, "He hated that old hospital bed. It was too short and narrow. Why, I could have just gone down to the furniture store and had them bring in a bed big enough for him."

There really was no help. Dad was gone; he was dead. He was never coming back. Childhood really did end there for my two brothers and me. We were not ready to be grown up, but we certainly could not be children any more. We had to go forward into a forced maturing. We entered with great speed into the rest of our lives.

Felix Goodson
1892–1936

The drought was there
when Felix Goodson died.
The air
was filled with silt
that cut the lungs
like shards of glass.
The land was bare
and all the grass
had blown away.

The cattle starved to bones.
The pregnant cows
began to slink their calves,
and they fell down.

The hands came then

with guns to give the mercy shot
and flensing knives
to take the hide.

When all were gone
my father's eyes
were dry as any bone
in that dry land.
And he lay down,
coughed out his lungs
and died.

Mother really didn't have time to mourn her husband. She had to begin her struggle to save what was left of the cattle. She had few resources. Dad had three thousand dollars of insurance money with which Mother bought the mortgage on his cattle. She had a savings account of her own with enough money to bury Dad, pay the hospital, and buy a new car. Dad's old car was almost worn out.

There was a little grass on the home ranch, but Mother wanted to save that grass for winter. She sent her herd south of Clayton. John and Felix and one cowboy trailed the cattle down by Hayden and left them there.

John was fifteen, and Felix was only thirteen. Felix could remember nothing about going with the cattle, but he did remember that he brought the horses back by himself. It took him three days to travel the eighty miles home. Three weeks later Mother and John drove down to see about the cattle. It had not rained, the pasture was bare, and the cattle were starving. John and Felix trailed the cattle back, losing several on the way.

Mother told me that the only time she ever almost

acknowledged defeat was when she saw the tiny herd come through the east gate. There were perhaps sixty head left. The big herd bull got just inside the home pasture and lay down and died. Nine cows died that night. There was some grass left in the canyons, and the scrub oak on the slopes of the mesa had leafed out, so there was enough forage for the rest of the summer for the small herd that was left.

Late in the summer, when the grass had finally all been grazed away and it was safe to fire the torch, Mother began to burn the cactus. Surely, torching cactus was a last, desperate measure. It was hot, dusty, and danger- ous. Mother pumped the kerosene tank full of air, then heated the burner over a wood fire. When she opened the valve to let the kerosene into the hot burner, the torch started with a roar that brought every cow on a dead run. Mother slipped her arms through the straps and pulled the five-gallon tank up on her shoulders. Then, holding the torch, which was shooting out a blue flame for a yard in front of it, Mother marched out into that frantic, milling herd of cattle and burned the spines off the cactus so the cattle could eat it.

Stella Goodson was a tiny woman, thin and barely five feet tall, but she had power. I said to Felix once, "And there stood Mother, towering under everyone."

He laughed and laughed. "My god, LaVerne, you've got her. That is exactly right; she did tower under every- one."

That is another ghost that haunts me. I can see that little woman in her sunbonnet and her apron, out there in that milling herd of cattle, their horns hooking at her. She walked backward as she burned the cactus, keeping the

flaming torch between herself and the cattle. It didn't
always work, and I have seen her dodge like a bullfighter.
Once she turned the torch on a charging bull and singed
the shaggy winter hair from one side.

Stella Goodson

1892–1977

In all that land
the only things that bloomed that year
were the tall white yucca bells
and the red wax roses of the cactus trees.
(Oh we should have gathered them
to dress my father's grave.)

Stella Goodson sent her sons
(Dear God, those stripling boys)
to trail her cattle down
toward rain
that had been rumored in the south.

But there was none.
The drought had tried
the water from those clouds.
The grass was gone.
My brothers brought the cattle back
a hundred miles through dust and wind.

My mother watched
as they came through the eastern gate,
then she rose up,
put her sunbonnet on her head.

> She strapped a tank of kerosene
> upon her back,
> fired the torch
> and flamed the cactus,
> bloom and thorn,
> to feed her herd.

At night, after supper, we all huddled closely around Mother as she tore apart Dad's clothes and pieced comforter tops from them. I saw her rip the seams in Dad's grey suit. That suit was almost worn out, but she blocked the grey pieces in with black squares, and they made a sturdy top. Dad had planned to run again for county commissioner and had bought a new brown campaigning suit. He was buried in that suit.

That summer Mother went into a period of compulsive thrift. She took my two brothers, my little sisters, and me, time after time, to gather windfall apples from the orchard at the Harris Ranch. Every time she saw a patch of lamb's-quarters—a sort of wild spinach—she made John stop the car. We all got out to pick the greens, which Mother took home and canned. From time to time we older ones tried to rebel against the gathering and picking, but Mother forced us to it.

I know Mother didn't mean to frighten us when she talked about our having to go live on the section line, and I really thought I was the only one who was terrified. But my sister Barbara told me once that she, too, had been scared to death of the section line, though she didn't know what it was.

In her childhood, Mother had seen families who had been evicted from their farms. These families had camped

on the right-of-way along the roads. They became to my
mother a symbol of ultimate horror.

The Section Line

"We'll have to go live on the section line,"
my mother said, and said again.

Anything that put such horror
in my mother's voice
was black enough to sweat me all night long.

I saw the section line,
a narrow place where we must perch
hungry, cold, and dispossessed.

I do not know the picture in my mother's mind,
or why the section line became
her metaphor for fear.

I know the fear was real enough.
A husband dead too young,
his get a heavy burden on her.

I have been told
there is no section line.
That's as may be,
but I am not convinced.

We all have got our strip of terror.
My sisters died on theirs,
my brothers age,
and I edge closer to a narrow line.

Mother never talked to us children about that summer after Dad died. We knew she was afraid and that knowledge frightened us, but we had an abiding faith that Mother could take care of us.

We got through it somehow. John and I went out of the Valley that fall into a world foreign to us. We were both seniors in high school and had to leave the Valley for that last year. I was packed off to Grandma Goodson in Muleshoe, Texas, and John went to board in Clayton. We went from a junior class of two to senior classes of dozens, for me an overwhelming experience. I learned about pep rallies, football games, school plays, and movies every Friday. I also learned that my only social grace was worthless. They didn't dance in Muleshoe.

John and I went to college the next year, and Felix went to Clayton. The year after that John married Norene and brought her to the ranch. I married Jiggs Collins and moved to Kenton. Felix joined the Army. Then World War II fell on all our heads.

The little girls grew up during that war. Barbara went to college, then got married. Virginia became a registered nurse, and she, too, married. I have not written much about my two younger sisters. They were really only babies when John and Felix and I were growing up. Then we were gone when they grew up. In truth, I can hardly bear to write about them now, for they grieve me terribly. Those beautiful, beautiful women were afflicted with the same sort of heart trouble that took Dad's life. They both, like Dad, died young. Virginia died at forty-five years of age, and within the year Barbara died at the age of forty-four. They left husbands and children and our poor mother, who survived this double blow because she had Barbara's two younger children to care for.

Mother was a survivor of the cotton fields of Oklahoma and the blizzard-swept flats of southern Colorado. The lessons she learned there brought her through her widowing and the loss of her girls. The drought, like the Great Depression, the cowboys, our parents, and that vast country itself taught us all to be survivors. We survived the war, although it took a toll on us. Jiggs joined the Merchant Marines, and that separation effectively ended our marriage. John and Norene were also divorced.

Fifty-six years have passed since Dad's death. Mother has been dead for fifteen years. Felix and Stella Goodson's children, grandchildren, and great-grandchildren have dispersed across the nation. My own children are scattered from Arizona to Michigan to Virginia, as well as New Mexico. My children grew up on the Goodson Ranch. They, too, know the secrets of the old Smylie place, the death-defying climb up through the chimney in the cap rock on the mesa behind the house, and the bank of purple shale that yields a new crop of fossils after every rain. There are only four of us left who know about the narrow canyon with the two giant trees. I do not know if Sandy, Jeanne, Kelly, or I could find our way back there now, for they are securely hidden. Susan and Nell saw the trees, but they were too young to remember them.

Walter found the trees quite by accident when he was trailing a two-year-old heifer. He followed her tracks where she had pushed through a scrub-oak thicket. He found her and her newborn calf under the most magnificent trees in all of New Mexico, if not the United States. They are red cedar trees, four feet thick at the base. They tower fifty or sixty feet into the air and are old, old.

Walter brought us all to see the trees. The canyon is really just a fissure in the side of the mesa. The trees are around a bend of the narrow canyon, shielded completely from sight. They took root in a small space where the canyon floor widened a bit and have flourished all these centuries in the only place where they could be safe. Kelly and I stopped and took photographs of the south mesas, and we both agreed on the location of the trees, but we swore ourselves to secrecy.

My children, especially the three older ones, do come back to the Valley, sometimes with me, sometimes alone. Kelly was just here in October 1992, and we drove to Kenton to have a hamburger and coffee in the little general store. Everett Like and Jack Matt Wiggins came in while we were there, and so did Bud Henry Davis, who told me Peggy was still alive and well. We talked and then went on to the cemetery and up the Valley past Battleship.

I probably will not drive down again by myself. Old age is troubling my eyesight, and I worry lest I be a danger on the highway. Perhaps when Kelly comes from Virginia next year we can visit the Valley again.

This time, while Kelly was with me, I wanted to go about to see once more the ruins of the brief civilization that flourished in the Valley between the two world wars. It was a separate and distinct civilization with its own codes and manners and, as with all civilizations, it left distinctive remnants.

Some of the ruins are personal. My hideout up above our ranch home is still there, but I am sure no one but me could tell it once was a safe haven carved out of the scrub cedar on the little ridge above the house. There are still mounds of dirt piled beside the white sandstone caves where Jiggs and I screened for arrowheads fifty years ago.

The rock walls of the old New Mexico schoolhouse still stand although they are crumbling now. The north wall is almost whole, and the blackboard is still there, chipped and cracked now and almost faded out. It was a simple blackboard, just black paint on a smooth plastered wall. The Valley School and the Wagner schoolhouse vanished with hardly a trace, but the Goodson School is still a solid building, although unused for many years.

I miss the houses. The Roberts Ranch and the Goodson Ranch have been restored, but many houses are empty or gone entirely. The Rutledge house has been torn down, and the foundations have been leveled. That wonderful long, cool living room with its huge fireplace within the north wall was one of the magical places of my childhood, and I am sorry for its destruction.

The old Behimer house burned down. Another house has been built on the site, but it is not the same. The old house was built beside the river and had a wide screened-in porch on the front. That house, too, had a long living room with a piano at one end. It was perfect for dancing.

I visit the ruins of the old homes and go up to the cemetery to read the names. I hardly know why I do this, but I think I am trying to find my way back to 1935, the year I was fourteen.

In July of 1935, we had been in the new house only a few weeks. Dad and Mother were persuaded to give a housewarming dance combined with a birthday dance for my fourteenth birthday. Dad invited every person in the Valley from beyond Kenton and up the Valley past the Likes. They were all there, including the young men who were too old to have been at the club dances. Charles

Capansky played the piano, and his cousin, Glen Capansky, played the guitar.

That dance was especially memorable because all the young people from one end of the Valley to the other came. There were Buddy Boy and Doug Layton from the canyons of the Cimarron River in Oklahoma. Rex Gillespie was there from the small valley across the mesas on the south. Jimmy and Jack Wiggins and the Capansky boys, Wesley Collins and his sister Evelyn, Virginia Jacobs and Oleta Layton, Betty and Milly Easley, Jiggs and David Collins, Laura Gay Quigg and Peggy Davis. Bud Henry Davis was there, and Everett Like, and Earl and Alvin Allen. Little Frank Layton was there and Junior Thorpe. The Behimers were there: Edna (the oldest girl), Velna, and Frank. There may have been others. I cannot remember any more, and there is no one to ask.

It seemed to me that if I could name all their names like a litany and seal them on this page, that wonderful time could be preserved forever. It would be the last time there were so many of us all together. Change was coming to the Valley.

But change was not yet, so we danced through the warm night, and fell in love, and agonized over who would walk us over to the refreshment table, or who would ask us to dance "Home Sweet Home." We were not yet concerned with the problems that plagued our parents. The war that was to involve our generation was only very dimly on the horizon, really visible only with hindsight. War, marriage, birth, divorce, and death were still ahead of us, and I think the children of the Valley were lucky to have had such a free and open childhood. We grew up snaky, fearless, and absolutely steeped in self-esteem.